10/23/04

A BIT OF HISTORY,
A BIT OF NOSTALGIA
AND A BIT OF
PERSONAL EXPERIENCE,

HOPE YOU LIKE IT.

FEATHER IN MY YARMULKE

FEATHER IN MY YARMULKE

FOND MEMORIES
OF AN INFANT ISRAEL

Marv Rubinstein

Schreiber Publishing
Rockville, Maryland

Feather in My Yarmulke

Marv Rubinstein

Schreiber Publishing
51 Monroe Street, Suite 101
Rockville, Maryland 20850
www.schreiberpublishing.com

Library of Congress Cataloging-in-Publication
Data

Rubinstein, Marvin.
  Feather in my yarmulke : fond memories of an
infant Israel / Marv Rubinstein.
      p. cm.
 ISBN 1-887563-80-6 (hc)
1. Rubinstein, Marvin. 2. Jews, American--
Israel--Biography. 3. Israel--Social life and
customs. 4. Israel--Biography. I. Title.
  DS113.8.A4R83 2003
  956.9405'2'092—dc21

                                      2003008950

Printed in the United States of America

DEDICATION

To the many friends with whom I shared my pioneering experiences in an infant Israel fifty years back. Some still live there, some have passed on and the rest are scattered around the world. I maintain contact with as many as I can. If you are still around to read this, I owe you all a debt of gratitude: Bea, Benny, Bob, Bracha, Dan, Esther, Hank, Irene, Jack, Kati, Lakey, Les, Lisl, Malka, Mike, Moishe, Paddy, Rachel, Rivka, Ruth, Sam, Sheila, Sol, Tibor, Zvi and a number of others whose names have unfortunately disappeared in the mists of memory.

Table of Contents

Over fifty years ago, the author spent three and a half years working for the Israeli Ministry of Defense. At the end of my third year, when I started planning to return to the United States, friends urged me to stay. "Israel needs people like you" was the constant refrain. "With your energy, your ideas and your skills, you can have a wonderful productive life here. You can be part of history. You can contribute to the development of a new country." I really gave it some serious thought, but eventually declined. As I explained to my friends, "Israel is a new country. There is a pioneering spirit. You are growing, building, advancing and, under these conditions, everyone is pitching in. It's exciting. But, as I see the future, in less than fifty years, Israel will become the equivalent of another American state, with all its pluses and minuses. I already have that, so why stay?"

Fortunately or unfortunately, depending on your point of view, my crystal ball was clear. Modern Israel could easily be absorbed into America as state number fifty-one. It is a true Democracy, though sometimes a raucous one. Its population is diverse and often contentious—just like ours. Tel Aviv is more like New York than London or Paris.

Though the country is basically secular, there is not really an absolute division between church and state, due to aggressive political activity by Orthodox Jews. But the same can be said about Mormon political influence in Utah. The standard of living is close to or perhaps as high as that in England. It is a very capitalistic consumer's society; you can buy almost anything in the shops. Energy levels are high, and ambition is rampant. The rush to make a shekel is parallel to our make-a-buck frenzy. Need I go on? Perhaps a bit more Levantine, but very much like a 51st state. For those readers who have not been to Israel recently, you will be amazed at what you see on your next visit.

I have made periodic trips to Israel since then, but half a century has passed, and time (and perhaps incipient Alzheimer) have taken the sharp edges off my memory. Still, I look back with warmth, fondness, chagrin and frustration at that extremely interesting and frequently entertaining period in my life. As noted, Israel has undergone several metamorphoses since then. It is a totally different place. But, like the father of a grown child, I still see it as it was a long time ago. The standard of living and the level of comfort were far below that of today, but the spirit—the SPIRIT—of the place was infinitely better. Everyone was pitching in to build a new and better country.

This book will not offer a sycophantic portrayal of the Country. There were many times during my stay that I threw up my hands and vowed to return to the States immediately for reasons you will clearly understand as we go on. Nor will it be a highly critical study, though there was and still is much to criticise. Think of this book as a concatenation of anecdotes and contemplative musings—some amusing, some historical, some geographical, some philosophical and some all of the above. Speaking of anecdotes, my stay in Israel reminds me of a story about New York City. A father from a small town in Virginia was visiting his son in New York. "Dad," said the son, "New York is dirty; the air isn't fit to breath; the traffic is impossible; the streets are crowded and harassing; the people are rude; and the town is expensive and sometimes dangerous." "Well, son," inquired the father, "when are you leaving?" "Leaving?" the son replied, "Who said anything about leaving?"

That is the way that many of us viewed Israel. With all its warts, Israel is a fascinating country—historically, culturally, gastronomically, politically—not to mention the fact that it is probably one of the two best places in the world for a tourist to see a great deal on a short visit.

And, fascinating as it is today, it was even more so 50 years back, when it had a real frontier quality, not quite like the Wild West in the United States, but with many intriguing similarities.

THE BEGINNING

The year was 1952. I was never a proper Zionist. Almost the contrary. While I sympathized with the plight of European Jewery, and was pleased to see the State of Israel created, I had absolutely no desire or inclination to leave my beloved New York City and spend my life building the land of milk and honey. True, I knew people my age who were avidly active in Zionist organizations such as Ha-Shomer ha-Tza'ir—some in dedicated preparation for emigration and taking part in the rebuilding of the Jewish homeland. Not I. In fact, none of my closest friends were part of that movement.

In a sense, I was not even a proper Jew. Genetically (since my mother was Jewish), culturally and gastronomically, I suppose "Yes," but religously, far from it. Having quit or been thrown out of three Hebrew schools in my early teens for asking too many logical but impertinent questions, I had never even been Bar Mitzvahed. I drifted into atheism at an early age, when I discovered that religious people were no better and no nicer than non-practitioners. Perhaps no worse, but no better. Harry Lauder, a once-popular Scottish comedian and performer, used to sing a disdainful song on this theme, describing a man who lied, stole and cheated six days a week. The song was called, "He goes to Church on Sunday, and that makes him an honest man."

The father of a friend vigorously disputes my conclusion. When we discuss a certain Mr. Shapiro, who is an openly Orthodox Jew, but unarguably an unscrupulous businessman and a tyrannical landlord, I am told, "Look. With religion, he is a crook. But, without religion, he would probably have become a murderer." Maybe so. In any case, I am drifting away from my subject. This book is about Israel, not about the author. Still, in a book based on personal experience, it is almost impossible to separate the observations from the observer.

Back to the early 50's. The State of Israel was in its infancy, less than three years old. I was a 30-year old Chemical Engineer, single, foot loose and between jobs. With the exception of a couple of short visits to Canada, I had never been outside the United States. Still, far away places with strange sounding names were apparently calling me. I had just signed a contract to spend two years overseas setting up a plastics plating shop in San Paulo, Brazil.

I had given my landlord notice, had visited Rochester, NY to say good bye to my parents, and was half packed to go, when I received a phone call canceling the project. A financial crisis in Brazil changed my entire life. Otherwise, this book would have been about memories of Brazil; I would probably have married an Hispanic girl and had three half-Brazilian children instead of an Israeli born wife and three half-Israeli (but very American) children. Fate is quixotic.

Sweet are the uses of adversity. At just that moment, I heard of an opening in Israel to set up an aircraft maintenance plating shop for the Israeli Ministry of Defense and promptly applied. It was a decision I have never regretted. Apparently, my credentials were satisfactory. They hired me, and I was soon off to the Middle East, with only a short stop in Paris as an appetizer.

If I had been a believer in omens, I probably would have changed my mind along the way. To begin with, I missed the plane on my first leg. Actually, I was at the airport thirty minutes before departure time but, in those days, you were required to get on a flight manifest at least 90 minutes before leaving. I was not on the manifest and, even though I had ample time to get to the gate, and I argued vociferously, I was denied access. Then, a second set-back. Returning to a Manhattan apartment which I had shared with an old flame, I found that she had made a date for that evening with one of my best friends. No way to start a journey. Though I made the plane on the following day, this cut down my Paris stay to one day. One should never visit this most beautiful of man-made cities for only one day, and particularly if you have never travelled abroad before. It was too damned frustrating.

The seven-hour flight from Paris to Tel Aviv was uneventful, but intriguing. Among Jews, Israel always had the reputation of being the land of milk and honey — an oasis in the desert. After flying over the lush green fields of France, Italy and Greece, what a disappointment! Looking down on Israel, as the plane approached Lud airport, where was the green oasis? Small patches of green here and there, but mostly sand and more sand.

I always knew that everything is comparative, but did not have it amply demonstrated regarding the Israeli terrain until, several years later, when I flew to Israel from the opposite direction. Starting in Bangkok, the flight traversed countries such as India, Pakistan and Iran.

Looking down from the plane's window, what met the eye were tens of thousands of acres of desert and dry seer land, with occasional green patches. Finally, approaching what is now Ben Gurion airport from the East, what does one see? Thousands of acres of green countryside dotted with some patches of sand—a veritable oasis in the desert. As noted, everything is comparative. It all depends on your initial outlook. It took me some time to understand that everything in Israel must be judged by the same comparative view.

Tel Aviv in the 1950's (Inset: Tel Aviv today)

Purim parade in the streets of Tel Aviv (circa 1950)

A STRANGER IN A STRANGE LAND

While Ben Gurion airport is not exactly a thing of beauty today, it is at least reasonably spacious. The airport where I landed was dinky and spartan, to say the least. After clearing customs and purchasing some local currency, I was met by a Ministry of Defense representative, who drove me along a decidedly unattractive route to a Tel Aviv hotel on Hayarkon Street, where I was to stay for a couple of days before being assigned to "permanent" quarters. Hayarkon Street, which runs along the shore, is presently the site of an extensive esplanade dotted with rows of glittery tourist hotels. At that time, however, there were only a few small and slightly shabby ones.

My hotel room was small as well, and the furnishings minimal, but the ambiance was pleasant. The windows opened on a seaside view. Since I arrived on a Friday, and the next day was Shabat, I was told to get some rest to overcome any jet lag, and that someone would pick me up Sunday morning. "Don't worry about language" was his parting comment. "Most people speak English." Strange to say, it was true, but more on language later on.

Saturday morning, after an early Israeli breakfast (vegetables and a type of yogurt called lebenia), I set off on foot to explore the town. Today, Tel Aviv is a lively thriving city. Forty five years ago, it was neither fish nor fowl. It was not like a Polish shtetl or a sleepy village. No town, village or city in Israel could ever be called "sleepy." But neither did it have a city ambiance.

Most streets were narrow, and irregularly paved, to say the least. Sidewalks were often broken, with missing portions exposing the underlying sand. Most buildings had the tired, neglected appearance common to seaside resorts constantly exposed to wind and salt spray and with insufficient capital for renovations and cosmetic improvements. Few buildings were over five stories, and almost all of these required traversing dark hallways and climbing stairs. Highrise buildings such as the Shalom Tower, which today looks out over the city, simply did not exist at that time, possibly not even in anyone's imagination. I later learned that more attractive buildings existed, but these were on the outskirts or in newer parts of the city, not within easy walking distance.

Since it was Saturday—the Sabbath—the main streets were relatively empty, with most shops locked and barred, and only a moderate number of automobiles, nearly all of which had seen better days. The waterfront area was more lively, however, mostly with young people gathered in noisy packs. There were numerous small refreshment stands or kiosks offering soft drinks (gazeuse) and local fast food such as humus and falafel. For the uninitiated, humus is a thick paste made from ground chickpeas, sesame, olive oil, lemon and garlic (quite tasty once you get used to it). Falafel consists of deep fried balls of mashed, spiced chickpeas. People on the street seemed cheerful and lively. Everyone was happy to provide directions in English whenever I found myself slightly lost.

Their clothing was motley. Except in the immediate vicinity of the hotel, not a tie was to be seen. Open shirts, slacks, shorts and sandals were ubiquitous. Virtually no elegance. Casual with a capital "C." For the most part, these appeared to be people determined to enjoy whatever juices life provided. Whether they were happy or not, one could sense their energy and vitality. Modern Tel Aviv, on a smaller scale, has a pace and a feel more closely allied to New York than to London or Paris. And the reverse is also true. A New Yorker feels more at home in Tel Aviv or in Hong Kong than in any other major cities in the world. Singapore, Rio and Paris may be far prettier, but New York and Tel Aviv are more dynamic. That is now, but even fifty years ago, I could sense the beginnings of kinship with my home city.

A pleasant surprise for this stranger in a strange land. On my very first day, I bumped into a girl I knew, the younger sister of someone I had known in New York. She too had only recently arrived. We spent a couple of hours at one of Tel Aviv's ubiquitous cafés, chatting over a cup of tea. However, when I asked to see her again, she told me that she was with her father, who was very Orthodox, and that he would not allow her to go out with anyone totally out of their religious circle. My first, but not my last, encounter with the contradictions of this world I never knew.

Early Sunday morning, I was picked up by a young military officer who, after an exchange of documents, drove me to what was to be my temporary home, an old but substantial building in Jaffa, about a fifteen minute drive south of Tel Aviv. The route, close to the shore, passed through areas which had obviously seen the shock of war. There were half-collapsed buildings, buildings which needed tearing down, piles of rubble and wide open spaces which had obviously been bulldozed. Since Tel Aviv was mostly Jewish and Jaffa at that time substantially Arab, what we drove through was obviously a no-man's-land—the site of previous battles. I was later to find, however, that there were still occupied abodes hidden behind the rubble in this area, and that these included a couple of small, dismal but very good Arabic restaurants.

Jaffa was a partially walled city, and we entered through what at one time must have been (but no longer was) an impressive gate. Inside, the streets were narrower and more crowded and noisy. In addition to cars, roadside traffic included bicycles, baby carriages, heavily laden donkeys, hand-pulled carts, donkey-pulled carts and heavy foot traffic. There were still plenty of slacks and shorts to be seen, but also large numbers of Arabs in traditional kaftans. A cacophony of automobile horns added to a variety of other street noises. A variety of street smells met the nose.

I was driven to the entrance of a military encampment, which turned out to be Machene Ariel, then the Central Headquarters of the Israeli Air Force. I had been hired by the Ministry of Defense, but most of my work was to be with the Air Force. After a lackadaisical security clearance at the gate, I was provided with a room on the third floor of an old but obviously solid and substantial building, originally the home of a well-to-do Arab merchant. It was similar to most of the buildings within the encampment, apparently once a prosperous neighborhood. The streets, sidewalks and narrow passageways were all paved with cobblestones. This was a hilly area, and navigating around it required energetic climbing. The whole place looked shabby to me but, had I had foresight, I would have bought real estate there (had it been available). Many years later, this encampment area was cleaned, scrubbed and renovated. It is now a lively Greenwich Villagey tourist area complete with shops, restaurants, boutiques and upper middle class residencies for artists and craftsmen. Unfortunately, the uniqueness of the neighborhood ambiance escaped me at the time.

My room was large and airy. There was no heating or air conditioning, since the building was designed with the local climate in mind. Floors were tiled and walls were very thick. Shutters enabled shutting out the intense Middle Eastern sun, into which only mad dogs and Englishmen ventured at mid-day. The thick walls and shutters did indeed prevent suffering from hot weather, but the theory that no heating was required in semi-tropical climes was simply that, a theory. In fact, as shall be noted later, during the rainy season, the walls absorbed moisture and, between the dampness and the stone tiled floors, one could begin to shiver, even though winter temperatures were not particularly low.

This was a military outpost and, even though many of the people housed there were foreign specialists or Air Force officers, the furnishings were at a college-dormitory level. A bed, a chest of drawers, a chair and table and a slightly uncomfortable comfortable chair—that was all. My escort left me on my own, and I spent most of the day wandering around the base and the building, getting to meet as many of my fellow luxury livers as possible. This included a motley group of other American specialists who had been hired at the same time I was. And it included two young

British "gentlemen"—Flight Engineer Sol and Aircraft Maintenance Mechanic Zvi—with whom I was later to develop a lasting friendship.

Members of the new Israeli Air Force during the 1948 War of Independence

THE MILITARY

I suppose that, at this point, I should be giving you my first impressions of the Israeli people. My first serious contacts, however, were with the Israeli Air Force and its members. They too were people, but a special breed. Never having had any previous military experience, I did not know quite what to expect when I was first introduced to the Tel Nof Air Force base, but certainly not what greeted my eyes. In one way, they were like the Saturday crowd on Hayarkon Street. Absolutely no spit and polish. Everyone was casual, in both dress and manner. Open shirts, no ties. Hats, if worn at all, askew. Boots covered with a light dusting of Israeli sand.

And their relationships to each other were as casual and informal as their clothing. Privates and officers freely mingled, always on a first name basis. There were few, if any, women pilots, but otherwise, I saw no evidence of male chauvinism in the ranks. And, in over three years of service there, I never saw a single salute.

Organization? What's that? In my lifetime, I have been active or seen activity in clubs, businesses, colleges and government. Believe me, I have seen loads of poor organization and disorganization. But the Israeli Air Force (and at a later date, the Navy, where I also worked) took the cake. Telephone communication was poor, as it was in all of Israel. Messages often had to be hand-delivered to an office at the other end of the base. Being late for appointments was the rule, rather than the exception. Schedules often had to be extended. Nothing was done in a timely fashion. In short, the military organization there was a mess.

When I later started to organize my plating workshop, I found a similar situation. Warehouses yielded a mishmash of materials, chemicals and equipment—old, new, in working order, repairable, useless, properly labeled, improperly labeled, with or without instruction manuals. Some of it had been left behind by the British army when they pulled out. Some new items had apparently been ordered by engineers or chemists temporarily assigned to the area. Many items defied guessing as to their origin. Amazingly enough, however, once everything was identified and relegated to its proper place, the makings of a respectable, working plating shop were all, or almost all, there.

What was true in my work area, I later found, was the rule rather than the exception for other military sectors, including maintenance materials, office equipment and even aircraft. I was later to find that some things were even worse in the civilian administration. But, over a reasonable period of time, it all seemed to come together. The chaotic element never completely disappeared, but working operations forged ahead. I recently read a book on the early history of Israel's intelligence community, only to find that the same inefficiency and confusion existed in that highly touted group.

Don't ask me how, but somehow, the system worked. This was a military force which, starting as a rag-tag army, had won its first war against overwhelming odds. They had been outnumbered by the Arabs more than twenty to one. Many nations refused to sell them arms. Their pilots dropped bombs manually over the sides of small aircraft. Lacking proper uniforms, many soldiers wore partial military garb, catch-as-catch-can. The chain of command had many missing links.

Yet, they won their war of independence and, years later, four subsequent wars against ever improving Arab forces. How does one account for this? One explanation is that they had zeal and spirit and were fighting for a dream— the first Jewish state in 2,000 years. Or because they had their backs to the wall and had no place else to go. Maybe they were brilliant tacticians or, bad as they might be, it is highly likely that the opposition was far worse. What is that old expression—the strong lord it over the weak and the smart lord it over the strong? The bottom line is that they succeeded, so my superficial initial diagnosis was obviously erroneous.

Immigrant youth working on a banana plantation

FOOD

An imported Ford Anglia with New York license plates and carrying three Westerners—one American, one English and one Scottish—drives into Nazareth. As soon as it stops in mid-town, an Arab wearing a burnoose approaches. "Maybe you like to buy something in my shop?" he asks, gesturing to a small store across the street. "Maybe," is the reply, "What do you have?" The Arab grins. "Beautiful brass items, carved olivewood, lace made by the nuns..." His voice lowers and becomes more conspiratorial, "chickens, eggs."

Variations of this scene occurred many times during my stay in Israel. Was there a shortage of food, which drove us on food hunting expeditions? Not exactly. Then, why did we do it? The answer is "tzena." A loose translation would be "austerity." Nobody starved, but there was not too much to savor. Vegetables were plentiful, but seasonal. When tomatoes were in season, every household and restaurant had numerous dishes which included tomatoes. The same applied to eggplant, a very popular local vegetable, which was often served as a meat substitute, since it had a meaty texture and taste. When in season, eggplant was on every menu. Greens and cucumbers were always available. A present day dieter living on salads would have found Israel seventh heaven.

Fruits were also available, with heavy emphasis on citrus. Jaffa oranges—a major export—were and are among the best in the world. There were plenty of grapes, which led to the early development of wineries in the country. Figs and dates were grown locally, as were some melons. A limited supply of apples and pears from the northern hills and of bananas from a Kibbutz on the Sea of Galilee periodically appeared on the market. Strawberries were seasonal and not easy to come by. In short, you could normally buy only commonly known fruits and vegetables. Today, almost any type of fruit or vegetable that can be grown in a a temperate or in a hot dry climate can be found in the stores. During my 3 1/2 years in Israel, I never saw a kiwi, but non-indigenous Israeli grown kiwis are now a major export item.

The main food problem was protein. Meat was definitely a luxury, and fish was in very limited supply. Chicken in limited quantities was sometimes obtainable, but eggs were severely rationed, as were milk, flour, sugar, coffee and tea. Since there were few cattle, almost all meat was imported. Cans of an inedible South African fish called Snook were occasionally on grocery shelves, but this was, well, inedible. The only other fish periodically available was a frozen fish filet called "dagfillet." This was much better than the Snook, but with a nondescript taste best described as boring. Meat had to be kosher, which further increased its cost. Israel is on the Mediterranean Sea, so that there should have been a plentiful supply of fish and sea food, but there wasn't. Israeli immigrants—mostly from land locked-areas of Europe and North Africa—had no cultural seafaring background. Many took readily to farming, but there was no fishing industry. Consequently, most fish were imported. Since shellfish are non-kosher, even if they had been available, their sale would have had to be sub rosa. To a young present-day Israeli, the fish shortage at that time would be wholly incomprehensible, since plenty of fish and seafood restaurants now abound almost everywhere around the seaside. As with many contradictory things in Israel, however, most of the fish served today still doesn't come from the sea. It has been "farmed" locally in inland ponds.

No problems with bread or with cereal grains such as oatmeal, though the bread had the color of sand and some-times tasted that way. Various dairy products were also easily available. In short, there was plenty to eat, but the daily diet was monotonous and uninteresting. One ate to live; only a privileged few lived to eat. Most desirable items were rationed. A few are mentioned above, but there were many others. Each household was granted a number of "nekudot" or coupons that enabled it to buy certain rationed items in limited quantities. The egg ration, for example, was one egg per person per week.

The restaurant situation was also pretty bleak. Outside of hotel restaurants, there was no such thing as an elegant eatery. Not that hotel restaurants were much better. Restaurants were small and spartan. Menus were relatively simple, without much variety. Service was, to put it mildly, kind of lousy. Many waiters in modern Israel have learned that efficient and polite service earns one bigger tips and insures a more substantial income. Not then. Many waiters had had more prestigious positions before emigrating to Israel. Some had been professionals or skilled technicians who now had problems finding jobs in their specialties. They needed the work, but considered the job of being a waiter subservient. Consequently, they made it abundantly clear in many ways that they were only there to make a living, not to kiss your "tochis." One could not even use the Hebrew term "meltzar" for waiter when summoning one. This would have been considered demeaning. Instead, one called out "Adoni," which translates as Sir or Mister.

The only saving grace were a few Arab restaurants or those run by Jews from North Africa. These were not particularly attractive in appearance, but the food was considerably better and the service at least tolerable. Salads were still the predominant items on the menu, but more varied and more imaginatively prepared. It took a while getting used to humus, falafel, hazilim salad, tabula and tahina (a thick sesame paste). These were all an acquired taste for a Westerner, but their quality was usually good. Today, falafel and humus are easily available in most large American cities. Then, there could be kabobs and sometimes fried fish. If you knew where to find them, there were even Arab restaurants serving shrimp and other sea food. Many travelled substantial distances to seaside Arab restaurants, where you could select and be served freshly caught fish.

Under these circumstances, food "delicacies" became something of an obsession, which led to many amusing situations, such as the one initially described in this chapter. For those with the means or the imagination, finding less available food items became a challenge—a kind of sport or mission. My friends Sol and Zvi and I spent many an evening and plenty of week-ends exploring possible food leads. For example, we discovered a Tel Aviv restaurant which, if you came just before closing, would sell you a bone "stew." After as much meat as possible had been cut away, the cooked bones were served to us so that we could gnaw away at any bits of meat still clinging to corners and crevices.

Rumors about obscure small Arab resturants in the most rundown sections of the Jaffa coast were relentlessly pursued, in the hopes of finding shrimp or fresh fish. Even the beer supply was erratic, with periodic dry spells. During one such spell, Sol and I were relentlessly seeking a bar or restaurant which still had beer available. After striking out at several places, we heard that there was a bar in Herzelia, about 10 miles north of Tel Aviv, where beer could still be found. Into the car and away. We found the place, and they still had beer, but when we arrived, the first person we saw there was Zvi, the third member of our triumvirate. Shades of D'Artagnan, Athos, Porthos and Aramis.

As a well-paid foreign specialist, I was able to import my own automobile. This gave us much greater mobility in foraging. Certain restaurants in Arab villages were almost always worth a visit. A particularly nice one was in a garden in Kfar Cana, a tiny village not far from Nazareth. There was always meat on the menu. We suspected we were eating donkey, but we never could prove it. In any case, hunger—real or psychological—made everything delicious. I remember that garden restaurant well, since you could pick your own hot peppers from a nearby bush. And boy, were they hot. On the outskirts of Akko, there was a restaurant well known to all of us food scavengers. It was called Abou Christo. You sat at long wooden tables in a dusty courtyard, separated from the sea by only a low wall. But you could go inside a ramshackled hut and select fresh fish from the catch of the day. These were substantial in size and, properly grilled, provided a veritable feast for those starved for protein. Abou Christo is still there, run by the son of the owner we knew.

Kibbutzim also provided excellent foraging spots. At that time, all visitors to Kibbuzim were welcome to stay for lunch or dinner. No payment was needed. (As time passed, with privately owned automobiles becoming more common and recreational Kibbutz visiting starting to flourish, payment or work was expected for your meal.) Like elsewhere in Israel, Kibbutz meals were heavy on salads and vegetables, but a few established a reputation for out-of-the-ordinary specialties. One in the North, Ein-Dor, mostly populated by Americans, had peanut butter available. Peanut butter? Would you drive miles for peanut butter? Well, we did. Psychological hunger can become an addiction.

Another Kibbutz on the Sea of Galilee was one of very few growing bananas at that time. Definitely worth a visit. Keren Kayemet land grants for Kibbutzim in Israeli included a requirement that they serve kosher meals. Pork was strictly prohibited. Still, a few highly secular Kibbutzim cheated. Well away from the Kibbutz center, and usually behind high fences (so as not to endanger their financial subsidies), they surreptitiously and illegally raised a small number of pigs. Pigs were easy and inexpensive to raise. They could be fed whatever was left behind on dining room plates or in the kitchen. And, for the non-religious, pork is tasty and nutritious. The existence of these small "pig farms" was a tightly controlled secret but, somehow, our espionage team sniffed out their existence, and we included them in our foraging expeditions.

An amusing anecdote about Kibbutzim and food. Every Thursday, I drove from Ramat Gan to a naval base north of Haifa, where I was lecturing on my engineering specialty. Another American named Moishe often accompanied me as far as Haifa, where he worked for a different Governmental agency. About two thirds of the way to Haifa, we turned right and, using a rough, narrow, winding road, headed up into the hills of Mount Carmel, where we knew of a Kibbutz with a small restaurant, one which always had eggs available for breakfast. The restaurant was run by a motherly American lady, who got to know us and was very friendly.

One particular morning, when we ordered our eggs, she advised us that there was also chicken available if we were interested. We were interested. Our breakfast that day consisted of two fried eggs, toast and a substantial portion of roast chicken. When we had finished and were wiping our lips, this wonderful lady asked if there was anything else we might want. Facetiously, I responded, "Well, the meal would be perfect if we could only end it with some hot tea and a piece of warm apple pie." Believe me, I was not serious. Pies in Israeli were a rare commodity. Various types of cake were common at bakeries, and occasionally a tart, but pie, never. So, Moishe and I were aghast, but delighted, when we heard the response. "You're in luck. It just so happens that my son and his family are visiting from America, and I baked two apple pies. I will bring each of you a piece." The Hebrew word for luck is "mazal" and, for two American expatriates, this was mazal indeed

The pursuit of gluttony was not limited to restaurants and Kibbutzim. It extended to the market place as well. I found a small grocery in Ramat Gan that had many cans of creamed corn on its shelves. Now, corn was not popular in Israel but, when consumed, it was always on-the-cob. Creamed corn was virtually unknown and, when a shipment of cans arrived, including creamed corn, nobody knew what to do with it. When I ran across this treasure trove, the cans had been sitting on the shelf for months. I bought four cans and, ten days later, returned for six more. The grocer asked me what I did with it, and I answered that it could be used as a vegetable or combined with milk to make a great soup. I should have kept my mouth shut. The next time I visited, most of the cans of corn had disappeared from the shelf.

Yams suddenly came on the Israeli market, and American housewives scrounging for something different were delighted. Local ladies had only used small pieces of yam as a flavoring for soups, in much the same way that American cooks use turnips. So, when yams appeared, American shoppers bought two or three kilos at a time. Naturally, there came a time when one of them was asked what she did with such large quantities of yams. The lady obliged by suggesting that baked yams were great, and that they could also be used as a vegetable. She too should have kept her mouth shut. Several other American shoppers nearby heard this answer and nearly exploded. They had been zealously guarding this information for weeks, knowing that once locals knew what to do with yams, the supply would dry up. Their fears were justified, and the American who had let the cat out of the bag became a pariah. The food wars were fought seriously, with no holds barred.

There were no gourmet grocery shops in Israel at that time but, if you could find them, there were a very few grocery stores with specialty items. It took me a long time to track down one that sold spices. It was a dark little store with a "zayde" behind the counter. He spoke no English, so we conversed in Yiddish. My Yiddish, I should explain, is facile but limited. I only learned it as a child to prevent my parents from talking Yiddish behind my back. No sir, I could never have allowed them to get away with that. In any case, the spice store owner and I got along famously in Yiddish, since the important words required were the names of various spices. He expressed amazement that a young American man like me should know the Yiddish names for so many spices. What he didn't know was that most spice names in English and in Yiddish are more or less identical. I was not about to tell him

This preoccupation with food of course led to gluttony. Just because there was less, human nature demanded more. When I first arrived in Israel, I was assigned a room in what was formerly an Arab mansion in Jaffa. The building was located in a military headquarters encampment, with its own mess hall, which is where several of us had our first breakfast of the day. This usually consisted of vegetables in lebania, bread, chocolate flavored oatmeal (!!) and very bad tea. I mentioned "first breakfast of the day," because many of us worked at Tel Nof, a military base about an hour's drive away. That base had its own mess hall and, well, one can get very hungry over an hour's time. Originally, we commuted in the back of a panel truck known as a gimcy (G.M.C.). After a few months, when my car arrived from England, I was able to drive to work, usually accompanied by several friends who were officers. Now, these gentlemen knew of an Officers' Club in Rehovot, about half way to our work, where you could not only get another breakfast, but where they usually served eggs. (So much for egalitarianism.) Many of us ended up with three breakfasts. So much for austerity.

Lest this sound like just the personal experience of a privileged few, believe me, it was not. True, those with transportation, money and connections did better, but much of the population was mesmerized by culinary boredom, and many had their own little schemes for alleviating this ennui. Certainly, for European and American immigrants, perhaps on a subconscious level, and to varying degrees, there was a food hunting frenzy abroad in the land.

There were also what I shall call reverse gluttony problems. As a guest in the homes of people who were trying to be gracious, you were often pressured to consume items you knew were in short supply. I remember having to say "No, no, no" vociferously to a host who insisted that I take sugar in my tea. I hate sugar in tea, but he thought I was just being considerate, not wishing to take advantage of his precious supply. These situations were not infrequent in the land of tzena.

Most foreign specialists working for the Israeli Government on two or three year contracts were not Jewish. To entice them, the Government had to grant special privileges, and this included extra nekudot for food purchases. These extra rations, while not exactly gourmet fare, were more extensive than those granted the average Israeli. Even though I am Jewish, as a foreign specialist, I was one of the privileged. In addition, since I had my own car, I was able to forage around the country for food items not easily available locally. Finally, Mama, in Florida, worried that her little boy might waste away, sent periodic packages of food and other niceties. I recall once receiving a can of

Dutch cocoa, and ruminating at the travels it had experienced. Probably grown in Indonesia, the raw cocoa was shipped to Holland, where it was processed and canned. The can was then exported to the United States, and eventually re-transported to me in Israel. Quite a journey.

The bottom line was that my apartment in Ramat Gan became famous, particularly with Air Force personnel with whom I worked. It was rumored that only the U.S. Air Attache had a larder superior to mine. Needless to say, I had no problem making friends in Israel—many, many friends. Some of this, I'm sure, was based on my charming personality.

One particular package I received had amusing consequences. Two items in short supply were toilet paper and decent quality washing detergent . Toilet paper was particularly difficult to find. Most Israeli toilets at that time had a nail in the wall from which hung torn pieces of newspaper. If you could not satisfy one end of the body, why should anyone want to pamper the other? So most of us used old newspapers to wipe our behinds. A standing joke was that this enabled you to educate both ends. That explains why I wrote my family requesting toilet paper and some detergent.

When the package arrived, it was evident that it had been mishandled. I opened the box and found that the detergent container had burst open, scattering its contents.

What a mess. Food cans could be washed, but the detergent had thoroughly penetrated the rolls of toilet paper. Waste not, want not. For several weeks thereafter, whenever I went to the toilet and finished the paperwork, I was also laundering my tush. A fitting ending for this chapter on food.

Arab children with a donkey

CLIMATE

T The climate in Israel, a subtropical country, has of course not changed perceptibly during the past fifty years. Still, the temperature range did affect my life during my stay. Strange to say, the coldest few days of my life were spent in Israel. It was not that the temperature was so low; it was due to a juxtaposition of a number of unfortunate situations. In the middle of the rainy season, it had rained for nearly thirty consecutive days. Most buildings in Israel are made of stone, sometimes coated with stucco. After such a long period of continuous wet weather, the walls were impregnated with moisture. Green mold could be seen on many inside walls, reminiscent of Biblical references to hyssop growing on walls. Add to this the fact that the floors were made of glazed clay tile, and the buildings, designed for warm weather, had no central heating, and you had the perfect prescription for intense discomfort. Cold, dank, clammy, shivery—all these words applied.

When I came home from work, I could not get warm, could not stop shivering. The dampness had penetrated into my bones. The best I could do was surround myself with electrical heaters, climb into bed, and cover myself with blankets, coats, robes, whatever was at hand. I was born and raised in Rochester, New York, so I know the meaning of "cold," but I have never before or since felt it so sharply. (When I speak of "surrounding myself with electrical heaters," that unfortunately is not exactly accurate. I was limited to one or at most two heaters. Any more than that, and the electrical fuses would blow, sometimes in my apartment and sometimes even in adjacent buildings. Power capacities at that time were anemic and erratic, always cutting out at most inconvenient times.)

Of course, I am describing an abnormal weather event. Every year has a rainy season, November through January being the worst months, but this thirty-day rain phenomenon was unique. Every bridge but one over the Yarkon river in Tel Aviv was either damaged or destroyed by flooding. I remember standing on a high point looking down on what used to be a road, observing only the luggage rack of a bus sticking out of the water. (Getting back to the subject of food frenzy, on the day of that flood, we had a major dinner planned for friends. Due to the flooding, we changed the dinner site and advised everyone by phone. Unfortunately, we were not able to reach one couple. That intrepid pair journeyed to my house by a lengthy roundabout way involving about twenty extra miles. When they found a note on the door advising of the change, they doubled back along almost the entire rout, and still walked into the house in time for dinner. Ah, food!)

Generally speaking, the climate was hot and dry. I have since lived in Bangkok, which is equally hot but very humid. Believe me, hot and dry is much better. In some areas of the country such as the Negev or Beit Shean, summer temperatures could easily exceed 100 degrees Fahrenheit, though Jerusalem, at the other extreme, would occasionally be treated to snow. Normally, most places were hot during the day—65 to 95 degrees F.—and relatively cool, sometimes cold, at night.

The problem was that all buildings had been made for use in the subtropics. As previously noted, walls were thick and windows provided with shutters to avoid the hot afternoon sun. The thick walls and the tile floors kept people relatively cool even during a summer hot spell. That logic failed when extraordinary weather provided intense rain or an occasional dip in temperature. On such occasions, central heating would have been welcome, but it didn't exist, except perhaps in top hotels and a few very wealthy homes. Portable electric heaters could be found in some places, but not in most.

Weather of course varied from place to place and depending on the season. Spring and Fall were best, particularly March and April, when vast carpets of spectacular wild flowers could be viewed while driving through the countryside. The anemones ("kalaniot"), often carpeting hundreds of acres of countryside, were particularly spectacular, so much so that a popular Hebrew song extolled their beauty.

One other climatic anomaly must be mentioned, the "hamsin" or sirocco. Normally, the wind blew from the ocean towards the land, mitigating somewhat the effects of the hot sun. During a few days of the year, however, there would be a shift in the wind direction, and it would blow from the desert towards the sea. These hamsin days were, to put it mildly, horribly uncomfortable. In addition to being mercilessly hot, the winds brought with them millions of particles of very fine sand, which penetrated door and window seams, making breathing difficult, and leaving each household the gritty task of cleaning up. I was told that, in accordance with some ancient Arabic laws, murders occurring during a sirocco could sometimes be forgiven, since the weather had obviously driven the perpetrator mad.

In any case, at most times, Israeli weather allowed us all to dress comfortably in shorts and loose tee-shirts, perhaps carrying a sweater for evening wear. And, following the advice of the British, whenever possible, we never went out in the mid-day sun. In tropical and semi-tropical climes, casual wear often becomes fashionable wear and becomes the accepted norm. In the Philippines, for example, the barong, a loosely fitting thigh-length shirt worn by men is acceptable wear at banquets, weddings and other formal celebrations. Similarly, in Thailand, a light cotton suit with a Nehru type jacket and short sleeves is sort of a national outfit. Even formal French restaurants, which normally require a tie and jacket, accept this outfit as dinner attire.

In Israel, a story is told about Prime Minister Ben Gurion who, having just attended a diplomatic meeting where striped pants and a cutaway jacket were de rigueur, had to hurry to address a conference of Israelis wearing their usual very casual attire. Not having had time to change clothes, he rushed to the rostrum but, before sitting down, apologized to the audience, "Please forgive me for having to come here in my work clothes."

BUREAUCRACY

Bureaucracy is the hallmark of government, academia and third world countries, and Israel is no exception, even today. Fifty years ago, it was worse. There was even a bit of bureaucratic legerdemain at the airport when I arrived. At the immigration check station, they would normally stamp your passport with an Israeli entry stamp, indicating the date of arrival.

What I did not know was that, if you so requested, the immigration officer would put the stamp on a separate piece of paper inserted into your passport. The reason was that, as part of the Arab League's economic warfare against the new state at that time, if you had an Israeli stamp in your passport, most Arab countries would refuse to admit you. This subterfuge was of tremendous help to business travellers who needed to visit other middle eastern countries as well as Israel. At that time, irrelevant, as far as I was concerned, but it was intriguing to learn about this some time later.

I encountered numerous examples of bureaucratic thinking during my stay. A favorite example involved a confrontation at the Post Office. I had written an air letter to the

States, but I wanted it to go Special Delivery (called "Express" in Israel). If any reader is not familiar with an air letter, it is a flat piece of thin paper with an adhesive lip, designed to be folded along certain lines and then sealed. In short, it forms its own envelope, and already has a printed stamp on one corner. Air letters provide a less expensive way to send overseas air mail.

I took the letter to the Post Office, waited in a long line (as usual) and asked to buy an Express stamp to adhere to my letter. The postal clerk looked at the air letter and told me, "Adoni, you cannot put an Express stamp on an air letter." Since I had done exactly that on previous occasions, I expressed amazement and asked why not. He patiently explained to me, as if I were a child, "Don't you see, Adoni, the printing on the air letter? It says that, 'Nothing can be inserted or attached to the air letter'." I laughed. "Adoni," I told him, "That refers to extraneous matter, such as extra sheets or tickets or receipts. It does not refer to Express stamps. One can always mail an Express air letter." He shook his head, "Where does it say that?" I argued that it didn't have to say that, that it was only common sense, and that I had previously mailed many air letters Express without any problems. He would not budge. I might just as well have been talking to the wall.

Shortly after I started writing about this episode, I was in a New York restaurant, when something caught my eye.

A small line at the bottom of the menu read, "We accept only American Express cards." I laughed, wondering what that poor literal Israeli postal clerk would have done if he had just finished eating at that restaurant, then noticed this notation, and realized that all he had with him was cash.

Back to the post office. I finally said to the clerk, "What am I supposed to do?" His advice: if I walked two blocks down the street, I would find a stationery store. I could buy an envelope, put the air letter in the envelope (thus wasting the value of the air letter stamp), seal and address it and bring it back to him. He would then sell me an air mail stamp and an Express stamp. I hit the ceiling. "Let me speak to your supervisor," I yelled. Note that, while all this was going on, a long and impatient queue was forming behind me.

The supervisor finally appeared. I calmed down and patiently explained to him that his clerk, from lack of knowledge, was making a mistake. All over the world, air letters can be sent Express, and that the restrictions printed on the air letter did not apply to Express stamps. Air letters were just a less expensive way of sending air mail of limited weight and, if one were willing to pay the extra charge, they could be sent Express just as regular air mail could. Another stone wall. He kept insisting that the printing on the air letter had to be taken literally. No exceptions. [Note: I have since double-checked post office rules on this, and he was wrong.]

Finally, in total exasperation, I warned him, "Adoni, if you do not sell me a stamp and allow me to mail this air letter Express, I shall drop everything I have to do today, go down to the Main Post Office, wait until I see the Postmaster personally, advise him of your ignorance of postal regulations, and issue a formal complaint against you." If I had obviously been an Israeli, my ranting would probably have fallen on deaf ears, but coming from a well-dressed and authoritative looking American, the threat must have seemed more ominous. "Wait,wait," he told me, "no need to get so excited. It is not a big deal. I will see to it that your Express air letter is mailed today." End of episode.

This may seem like a silly episode on both sides, but it was typical of frustrating impasses one encountered on a regular basis, particularly when dealing with Israeli Governmental agencies. Lest the reader think that the above encounter is unique to Israel, however, rest assured that it is typical of many third-world countries, and even occasionally in the United States. How to explain the frequency of such skirmishes in Israel? Well, for starters, Jews tend to be opinionated and contentious (as do most inhabitants of Mediterranean countries). Perhaps not all Jews, but a substantial percent of the population. One need only read about Israeli politics to become aware of this. An old joke claims that if you have three Jews in a room, you have four political parties.

Perhaps more important, Israel was a new country, with the need for a variety of skills and experience. As mentioned earlier, many immigrants, particularly those from Europe, had been professionals or skilled technicians in their homeland. When they arrived in Israel, they found that there were not enough jobs in their particular skills to go around. Consequently, they had to take what was offered and learn while on the job.

What was offered by a new Government, particularly for white collar workers, was a growing number of clerical and low and intermediate level administrative jobs of a bureaucratic nature. Many reluctantly accepted their new positions but, once ensconced, fought like tigers to hold them. Confessing to lack of knowlege or skill in what they were doing would be an admission of defeat. They had learned to act in a self-assured manner in their previous occupations, where they had some expertise, and could never shake the habit of self-confident confrontation in areas where their skills were limited or nonexistent.

Lack of confidence in the ability to do one's job properly also makes one supersensitive to any form of criticism, large or small. I remember going to the Licensing Bureau for a driver's license. There were four windows, with a large number of people lined up at three of the windows where a sign read, "Drivers' Licenses." The fourth window, marked, "Truck and Commercial Licenses," had no queue. After an interminable wait, I marched over to the fourth window, where the clerk sat twiddling his thumbs. I asked him, since there was such a big crowd, and since his window was empty, why he didn't take care of those who were seeking drivers' licenses. His manner became surly. Assuming from my accent that I was an American, he snarled at me, "Adoni, why don't you mind your own business. This is the way we do things here. If you don't like it, go back to your own country."

Reinforcing this was a type of cultural bias, particularly for those who had emigrated from Eastern Europe. As one friend from Romania told me, "Marv, you come from a country where, when you file your annual taxes, you normally pay the entire amount due. If I had done that in Romania, the tax clerk would have assumed that I was flush with money and consequently had to be cheating. I might get called in, but even if I weren't, my tax bill for the next year would have been larger. Once you get used to that idea, you never pay your taxes in full. You make a partial payment, write a letter pleading poverty, and pay the balance in installments." This type of mind-set makes citizens suspicious of their Government and Government officials suspicious of those with whom they deal. Even when it comes to postage stamps.

Even in the military—or perhaps particularly in the military—bureaucracy also reared its ugly head. I was working for the Ministry of Defense setting up electroplating shops for the Air Force and the Navy. Electroplating baths require relatively pure water, and the water around our maintenance facility was very hard, containing a high concentration of minerals. A piece of equipment known as a demineralizer was required to remove these minerals. The demineralizer could be ordered from the States, or I could design and have one built in Israel more cheaply and with less delay. In either case, we needed to have the local water analyzed.

I had no doubts that such analyses were available locally, but I decided to send a gallon to a U.S. firm which specialized in manufacturing demineralizers. The reason was that, not only would they analyze it for free, but they would also quote me on a proper installation, with full details about dimensions, capacity, etc. Though I had already decided to have the unit built in Israel, these specifications would save me loads of time in providing a proper design. So, I packed up a gallon of water, attached an accompanying letter, and took it to the Transport Officer with instructions to send it by air to the American demineralizer manufacturer. He promised to do so.

A month passed and, not having heard from this company, I went back to the Transport Office to inquire as to when the bottle had been sent. To my surprise, what did I see sitting next to the officer's desk, but my bottle of water. I was furious. One whole month wasted, and I was still unable to complete my project. When the officer returned, I upbraided him, demanding to know why the water had not been shipped. He referred me to his superior, who had apparently told him not to ship it. Of course, no one had bothered to advise me of this decision.

His boss was only marginally more cooperative than the officer with whom I had first consulted. He plied me with false logic. "Marv," he said, "why don't you have the water analyzed here? We have very competent chemical laboratories." When I explained that I knew about local analytical facilities, but there was a larger question of getting the U.S. supplier to provide me with specifications and additional data, he remained adamant. "Look," he pleaded, "what will the Americans think of us if we send them a bottle of water for analysis? It would be demeaning. They would think we were a backward third-world country, with not even the ability to analyze water." In short, it had become a matter of face saving which, in its own way, proved self fulfilling; Israel at that time, was undoubtedly a third-world country.

Face saving is extremely important in the Far East and in third world countries. I once sold a piece of engineering equipment to Malaysian Lines. The sale included the services of an expert who could get them started. Because I was well-known in the field, the head of their maintenance department "requested" that I come. I tried to beg off, advising him that I was just too tied up at the time. I offered to send them my top instructor. This led to my receiving a furious letter, "Do you think that we are just a two-bit country, who could be satisfied with second rate service? We deserve the exact same treatment you give to companies in America or England." They demanded that I personally make the trip, since I was the top expert in the field. Malaysia is a long way from Israel but, in certain respects, the third-world psychology was not too different. It took me quite a while to understand that this was one explanation (but not the whole one) as to what contributed to some of the bureaucratic problems I encountered.

Returning to my water shipment problem, I had to go over this officer's head and, only at an upper level, after an extended argument, was I able to have my water shipped out for analysis. In this case, it was only personal and national pride which made a simple task seem difficult. On other occasions, it was a subconscious fear of losing one's job. It was and is always easier to go strictly by the rule book and say "No," than to do one's job properly, carefully consider a request and then say, "Yes." If you say "No," and anything goes wrong, you can always claim you were only following the rules. In my eyes, doing one's job properly requires flexibility and understanding as well as a knowledge of the rules.

I remember an incident that occurred many years later in Ethiopia. I was travelling from Greece to Israel, with a business stop in Addis Ababa. While in Greece, I purchased a Turkish cheese called Kashkaval, a favorite of my then mother-in-law in Israel. When I checked into my hotel in Addis, I requested that the cheese be refrigerated for a couple of days until I left. Departure day, I asked for the cheese, only to be informed by the hotel manager that a mistake had been made and that someone else had taken the cheese. Since Kashkaval was not available in Ethiopia, he offered to have the hotel pay for my loss. The question was how much.

I went to a nearby bank to find the official exchange rate between Greek drachmas (which I had used to pay for the cheese) and Ethiopian Birr. The bank clerk looked up the figure and gave it to me verbally. When I asked him to write the figure down on bank stationary, since the hotel manager wanted it in writing, he hemmed and hawed. Finally, he turned me over to his superior, where we repeated the same rigmarole. He was happy to provide the exhange information verbally, but not in writing. I argued with him, telling him that he was not providing secret information, that the rates are posted daily by international currency organizations.

Believe it or not, I had to work my way up the chain of two bank clerks and two bank officers, before I found one with the confidence to fulfill my simple request. This same "safer to say 'No' than 'Yes' attitude" was not at all uncommon in the bureaucratic reaches of Israel. Always cover your ass. (In all fairness, while not to the same extent, I have encountered this in U.S. Government agencies as well.)

One bureaucratic mix-up almost landed me in jail. I was driving a small car I had imported from England under condition that I ship it to the States on completion of my contract. I had it registered in New York, and it bore New York license plates. What I didn't know was that the law only allowed you to use foreign plates for a six month period, after which you were expected to obtain Israeli registration. However, there was a Catch 22 situation. You could not register the car in Israel unless you had legally imported it and paid ridiculously high import taxes. And you could not legally import it unless you had an official import license. And, since the Government was trying to avoid foreign currency expenditures, you could not get an import license unless you could prove that you were a hardship case and desperately needed a car for reasons of health or a very necessary occupation.

None of which would have bothered me had I not been pulled over by a policeman and given a ticket for lack of proper registration. Once I got this ticket, however, the fat was in the fire. If I paid the fine, I would still be subject to an unpredictable number of additional fines until I registered the car in Israel. But I couldn't register the car because I had not legally imported it for a permanent stay in Israel. And I couldn't get legal import documents without an official import license. And I couldn't get an official import license due to stringent currency restrictions. Catch 22!!

So, I contested the ticket in court before an unsympathetic judge, who ordered me to pay the fine. Frustrated by the total lack of logic in a situation which left me no way out, I became obdurate. I told the judge that I would not pay the fine. I was not going to stop using my car, and I was not going to open myself to fine after fine after fine. Unless he could find a solution to my dilemma, I was prepared to go to jail rather than pay the penalty. As I suspected, the judge did not want the notoriety of jailing a foreigner in this impossible situation. The local newspapers would have had a field day. Furthermore, I would have missed work which the military needed to complete a project.

The judge's Solomonic solution was to have his clerk summon someone from my employer, the Ministry of Defense. They paid the penalty in spite of my very vigorous protests, and assured me that any future fines would be treated the same way. Much easier than trying to solve the basic problem.

Bureaucracy was of course not limited to governmental agencies. On a smaller scale, you could find it everywhere. Small stores with stubborn proprietors provided typical examples. I remember a Tell Aviv food market which, because it handled certain special items difficult to get elsewhere, found it profitable to advertise in the Jerusalem Post, Israel's English language newspaper. Included in the advertisement was a notation of the store's opening hours, namely from 9:00 A.M. to 6:00 P.M. At that time, I lived in Ramat Gan, about twenty minutes away.

One afternoon, I was a little late getting home, so I drove like mad to get to the store on time. I arrived at 5:40—twenty minutes to spare. However, while I could see customers still inside, the door was locked. I knocked vigorously and, after a while, a young lady came to the door, signalled that they were closed, and disappeared. I continued knocking, and finally the manager appeared. He opened the door slightly and told me that they were closed. "Look," I told him. "Your newspaper advertisement says that you are open until 6:00 P.M. It is only 5:45, and I have driven a long way to get here. Let me in." Without budging, he explained to me that they did serve customers until 6:00 P.M. but, when there were enough customers in the store, they would lock the door, so that the employees could serve those already inside and be ready to go home by 6:00 o'clock. Sophistry mixed with bureaucracy.

He finally let me in, but my argument that he was guilty of false advertising fell on deaf ears, as did my suggestion that he change the ad time to 5:45 or pay the clerks for an extra fifteen minutes. I managed to buy the food I wanted, but the girls behind the counter were sullen as Hell. If his shop is still there, I doubt if the policy has changed.

Probably the most traumatic of bureaucratic abuses arose when an Israeli wanted to leave the country. I had married a Sabra and, when I wanted to take her back to the States with me, I experienced this fiasco firsthand. For starters, she needed to obtain an Israeli passport. For a U.S. visa to travel to the States as my wife, the passport had to be in her married name. For this, she needed a civil marriage license from a small Israeli office with limited visiting hours.

The certificate of marriage we had obtained during our religious nuptials was not sufficient. That marriage was only officially recognized in Israel. In the United States and other western countries, one can obtain a legal and binding matrimonial license at a County Clerk's Office. Or you can get married by a Rabbi, Minister or Priest with confidence that your union is legal. These religious leaders are officially licensed by the government to perform marriages, and their signatures on documents are official by both religious and civil standards. But not in Israel. You could live there for the rest of your life as a married couple but, if you wished to travel overseas with an Israeli passport, you required a civil certificate as well.

For two friends of mine, Sam and Sheila, this provided material for an amusing story. They were both British citizens, but had been married in Israel. Periodically, they visited and stayed with her parents in London. Since they both travelled on British passports, they did not require a civil marriage certificate to obtain documentation. Sam used to enjoy saying good night to Sheila's parents in the living room and, while he and Sheila were climbing the stairs to the bedroom, grinning down at her parents and saying. "You know, of course, that in England, Sheila and I are not legally married."

Having procured her civil marriage license, my wife's next step was to apply for a passport in an entirely different building in an entirely different neighborhood. Incidentally, none of these document applications was a one day step. It required one trip to obtain the application blanks. Since there were many, many questions, one normally had to take the form home to fill it out and go back the next day to file it. You were then given a third date to pick up your passport.

Weeks later, passport in hand, my wife then had to go to a third office to request an Israeli exit visa. Exit visas were at a premium, since foreign travel almost always involved hard currency expenditures—admitted or concealed—and the powers that be were bound and determined that such travel be limited to special circumstances. Being married to me was a special circumstance, but that didn't mean that the issuance of an exit visa was automatic. Some bureaucrat had to probe and question at length to determine that no monkey business was involved. One needed to bring a religious marriage certificate, a civil marriage certificate and other documents, as well as filling out several lengthy forms. Now, one would think that, if several forms had to be filled out, the applicant would be given all of these initially. Wrong. You normally received one form and, after you had filled that out and returned it the next day, you were given another, etc., etc. No one could or would ever explain to me why the applicant couldn't get all the forms at once. "This is the way we do things here."

In my wife's case, however, there arose a special problem. One of the required documents dealt with finances. The Government had to be assured that you were not leaving behind any debts when you left for overseas. This included personal debts as well as governmental ones, though I have never understood why the Israeli Government, with all of its other problems, needed to concern itself with the personal or commercial non-governmental debts of an individual, unless of course the purpose was a make-work program for bureaucrats. On a return visit to this office after the financial form had been returned, my wife was dumbfounded to learn that she could not be given her exit visa until she paid off a large debt to a department store, a debt which she swore she did not owe. It seems that someone with the same maiden name as my wife owed that debt, but proving a negative became onerous, time consuming and frustrating enough to make one's hair stand on end.

If the reader finds reading this section tedious, try to imagine the emotional drain of anyone trying to penetrate this bureaucratic thicket. It took more than two months to complete, with hundreds of hours sitting and waiting in various offices, all with limited visiting hours. God forbid that you arrived just before a clerical tea break. Did I mention that many of these offices were distant from each other?

After all of this, getting her visa to enter the United States, while not without its own bureaucratic hurdles, was easy as pie—apple pie.

Bukharan Jewish family celebrating Hanukkah in Israel

RELIGION

While Israel is always referred to as a Jewish state, it is essentially secular, and was even more so fifty years back. Most European Jews who first settled there were politically socialists and spiritually non-practitioners. They never denied their Jewishness and, while large numbers held Seders on Passover and attended religious services on high holidays, and almost all had their sons Bar Mitzvahed, their way of life was essentially secular. They thought of themselves as cultural, philosophical, historical and perhaps even gastronomic Jews, but certainly not dedicated to religious practice and rites. Their attitude towards their more Orthodox brothers was essentially "live and let live," as long as that sentiment was reciprocal. Unfortunately, it wasn't. For reasons to be explained later, certain governmental departments dealing with religion and education came under the strict control of Orthodox Jewish political parties. This led to a degree of bitterness which, though rarely bordering on violence, continues to this day. Such control of highly visible areas of daily life in Israel unfortunately gave the appearance internationally that religion dominated Israeli politics. Not true, but there were problems.

Orthodox Ministers in the Cabinet dealt with all matters involving religion. One early problem. The Israeli Law of Return allowed all Jews who so desired to return to Israel and become Israeli citizens. But, who is a Jew? This question has never been satisfactorily answered by Israelis or internationally, but the Orthodox administrators provided a very narrow definition indeed. If your mother or your grandmother was Jewish, you qualified for the return. Otherwise, not. Someone who had a Jewish father and a Christian mother, even if raised in the Jewish faith, did not qualify.

What about those who converted to Judaism? If the conversion had been carried out by Orthodox Rabbis using a burdensome and time consuming procedure, you were considered Jewish. However, if you had undergone conversion by a Reform Rabbi or a Conservative Rabbi overseas, you could not make that claim. There were in fact only Orthodox Rabbis in Israel at that time. Even today, there are very few Reform or Conservative congregations in Israel, and they have had serious difficulties getting government authorization to perform marriages or arrange for burial of the dead.

Intermarriage is not legal in Israel unless the non-Jewish party first converts; if you want to marry out of your faith, you must travel to Cyprus or elsewhere. And, as previously mentioned, all marriages are religious. If you need a civil marriage certificate for reasons of travel, for example, you must get one from a special office after your religious marriage.

While I lived in Israel, there were few, if any, black Jews. Years later, when remnants of the Falasha (Ethiopian Jews) were airlifted to Israel in substantial numbers, this created another schism between the major party and its Orthodox coalition partner. The Government's position was that the Falasha were Jews and were entitled to return to Israel as part of the ingathering of the exiles. Orthodox party leaders (particularly the Ashkenazim), most of whom were innately conservative, did not consider them proper Jews. This was one quarrel where the majority view prevailed. Incidentally, the Falashas do not like the term "Falashas," which means "strangers" in Ethiopian. They always refer to themselves as the "House of Israel."

Incidentally, I once visited a small Falasha village in Ethiopia. A group of children there spoke to me in Hebrew and took me to meet their teacher, who was also their Rabbi. The Rabbi, after having the children do a hora in my honor, took me to see the synagogue, a small thatched building with a humble exterior. He proudly showed me the Ark where the holy scrolls were kept. Finally, he asked me to sign their guest book. When I looked at the book, there was a column for my name and one for my address. When I saw the third column, I knew I was back home again. It was marked DONATION.

Getting back to religious problems, some of the smaller inconveniences involving religious interference in everyday life were more troublesome than the major issues described above. Movies and places of entertainment were closed from sundown on Friday to sundown on Saturday. Buses were not allowed to run. Except in hotels, most restaurants were closed, and hotel restaurants could only serve cold dishes, since lighting a fire during the Sabbath was strictly forbidden.

At military facilities, the Saturday lunch often consisted of cholent, a slowly baked meat, bean and potato dish placed in the oven before sundown on Friday and cooked overnight without human attention. If you were served eggs instead of cholent, the whites were a dark brown, since the eggs had been slowly boiled overnight the same way. Many elevators ceased operation, unless they were engineered to stop at every floor without anyone touching the call buttons. Taxis were few and far between and, if you drove your car through an Orthodox neighborhood such as Bnei Barak, you could expect to have your windows smashed by stones thrown by Hasidim.

All this sounds very onerous. It really wasn't. A few disturbing stories regularly appeared in the press about couples traumatized by unjust interpretations of marriage rules, but the Saturday blue laws were more a weekend menace. We non-believers constantly kvetched about them. However, there was little we could do to change things. We consequently sought ways to avoid the problem. Since I had my own car, several friends and I regularly left Tel Aviv on Friday afternoons to explore the countryside, archeological sites, Arab villages and friends at non-Orthodox kibbutzim. We of course took pains to avoid driving through towns or streets with heavily Orthodox populations. We cursed these detours, but it was frustration rather than hatred that pushed our buttons.

The passage of time has to some extent mitigated the "minor" oppression of the religious parties. Buses now run on Saturdays in much of Israel. Many movies are open. Non-kosher restaurants are available in many areas. The Saturday closing laws, while still there to some extent, have become less oppressive. Those wishing to intermarry have found ways to do so, and problems involving the question of Jewishness have been partially solved through court intervention. There is still some stone throwing.

The biggest problems may lie in the future. Orthodox families tend to be much larger than secular ones. Since my time in Israel, once copious immigration (mostly secular) has decreased, while the proportion of religious Jews slowly but steadily has increased. (Higher birth rates have also resulted in an increase in the number of Arab Israelis.) Fifty years from now, some of the same problems as those

of fifty years back may recur. The seriously Orthodox
have not changed their tenets. They have learned to look
the other way, but only as a temporary bow to present
reality.

Incidentally, while Sabbath and holiday closings theo-
retically applied to all residents, it was not enforced in Arab
areas. Unlike many of its neighbors, Israel has always allowed religious freedom to Muslims, Christians, Hindus,
Buddhists and followers of all other religions. Even today,
while there is rampart anti-Arab sentiment because of the
suicide bombings, the hatred engendered is mostly against
Arabs, not Muslims. It is political and ethnic rather than
religious.

Ethiopian Jewish child receiving instruction

POLITICS

As a temporary resident hired on a three-year contract, I was never particularly affected by the machinations of Israeli politics. However, for the reader to get a true feel for the country, at least an elementary knowledge of the political scene is required. Long, sometimes highly contentious political arguments were heard in cafés, on the street, everywhere. I repeat an old Israeli joke: When two Jews get together, they form three political parties.

On the Israeli political scene, the more things change, the more they remain the same. Political turmoil was not much different fifty years back than it is today. If you think American politics is rough and tumble, believe me, it is nothing compared to politics as practiced in Israel then and now. Like people in many lands which were previously part of the British Empire, the Israelis, while they may have hated the British, inherited and took advantage of the infrastructure the British left behind. In addition to roads, bridges, power lines and water and sewage facilities, this included a Parliamentary form of democratic government. Under a Parliamentary system, you do not elect a President.

David Ben-Gurion, founding father and
first Prime Minister of Israel

Using proportional representation, you elect a group of legislators to a 120 member Parliament which, in Israel, is called the Knesset. Knesset Members then choose a Prime Minister, who presides over the Government and serves at the pleasure of the majority. More recently, the laws were temporarily changed to provide for direct election of the Prime Minister. David Ben-Gurion was Prime Minister during my stay. Oh yes, there is also a President, but his position is ceremonial only.

Knesset members are elected for four years and come from many different political parties. Parties change from time to time, but there always seems to be a plethora of them, including one or more shades of liberal, conservative, orthodox religious and Arab parties. The Prime Minister is selected by the majority party, providing they have at least fifty percent of the Knesset members, enough to create an operating Cabinet. Since there were over twenty political parties, and about twelve of them garnered enough votes (at least ten percent of the vote) to be represented in the Knesset, no single party has ever had a majority of the seats. This was true fifty years back and is still a problem. Consequently, all Israeli Governments since 1948 have been coalition governments.

The Mapai (a center left party), the Mapam (a left wing party), the General Zionists (a party of small merchants, mostly from Eastern Europe) and Herut (the conservative party) were the four main powers at Israel's inception. Mapai held a plurality of seats. Over the years, changes and mergers have occurred. Mapai has segued into the present Labor Party; the General Zionists and Herut into the present day Likud; and Mapam deteriorated into a less important group, now called Meretz. The Labor Party and Likud (today's arch rivals) are roughly equivalent to our Democrats and Republicans. Since, short of brief periods of military emergency, neither of these two can possibly coalesce with the other, coalitions almost always consist of one major party joined by one or more religious parties and, sometimes, by an Arab party. (About 15 percent of Israel's population is Arab.) This has always created many complications. Minority parties always insist on some type of power sharing as a reward for joining the majority. This normally results in the Religious parties getting Ministries which control religious practices and education.

Since education in the strictly religious schools connected with synagogues and their respective congregations was under control of the Orthodox, and since Orthodox leaders also exercised considerable influence on education in general, all public schools included biblical and some religious education as well as traditional secular subjects. One would think that children educated in these schools would graduate with an Orthodox bent. Certainly, most children at religious schools in Saudi Arabia become strong Wahabi adherents, but this did not happen in Israel. Most children from secular families remained secular, and those from Orthodox homes remained Orthodox. The reasons are difficult to pin down. Most teachers outside of the rabbinical schools had secular leanings, and the secular tendencies of student homes and in the streets probably negated any religious pressures from the school curricula .

The Orthodox Cabinet Ministers in charge of religion insisted that many religious rules and practices become part of our daily life. During my time in Israel, Kashruth was de rigueur in restaurants and in meat and fish markets. An attempt was made to shut down all activity except rest and prayer during the Sabbath. Movies and places of entertainment were closed. Public transportation (except taxis) was suspended. All public offices were closed. These restrictions also applied to most national holidays, since National and religious holidays are, with few exceptions, the same. Women and men were seated in separate sections of the synagogue, and modest dress was required of women worshipers. Only Orthodox religious practitioners received Government authorization and support.

With reference to holidays, strange to say, one of the things I missed most during my stay in Israel, was the celebratory nature of American holidays. In my eyes, Jewish holidays are, for the most part, dreary in nature. Yom Kippur (the Day of Atonement) was totally serious, since it is the day we are expected to pray for forgiveness of the sins we have accumulated during the year. Think of it as equivalent to the accumulation of fifty-two weeks of confession and penitence among Catholics. Rosh Hashanah (New Year's day) would seem to be more fun but, as part of a week of prayer, it too didn't seem very lighthearted. Many other holidays were somber, since they commemorated historical injustices to Jews. Pesach (Passover), while it also concentrated on chronicled troubles, was much more pleasant. Only Chanukah (the Feast of Lights) and Simchas Torah were celebrated with joy and levity, but mostly for children. Contrast these with the whooping and hollering and overeating and overdrinking of many American holidays, and you will get a sense of my craving for the carnival nature of American holidays.

As previously noted, the restrictions described above created a great deal of annoyance and loud vocal discussions among secular Israelis but never became a dangerous bone of contention in the political arena. There were, however, areas of religious control which did create political dissent between the party in power and its Orthodox coalition partners, some of it vigorous and rancorous. There has never been a meeting of the minds regarding fair distribution of available public funds to support both public schools and the more religiously dedicated Talmud Torahs. As a state surrounded by Arab enemies, Israel early on passed a law requiring all Jewish Israelis to provide a term of military service. This included women as well as men, though not all activities were open to women.

The Orthodox parties balked at having their women do military service. The general public was sensitive to this issue, so there was little active debate. However, the Orthodox parties insisted that young men who were dedicating their lives to the study of the Torah also be excused from military service. Their coalition partners eventually agreed to this in order to keep the coalition together, but not before extensive bitter and rancorous debate. Even today, this is a bone of contention, since most Israelis understandably consider it unfair.

Many of the earlier immigrants were labor Zionists so that, when the political structure of the State of Israel was established, early political control was seized by the Mapai Party, a left-leaning group with roots in Socialist principles. The Government was closely associated with a very strong labor union movement called the Histradut. In fact, much of the leadership was almost interchangeable, and very little could be done on Government policy without Histradut backing or agreement.

To say that discussions in the Knesset were lively is indeed an understatement. British Parliamentary meetings are much more contentious than most American House and Senate sessions, but the contentiousness of Knesset meetings surpasses both. Discussions are heated, raucous, impolite and bad tempered. Short of physical violence, no holds are barred. I observed a couple of Knesset sessions and was amused by the circus atmosphere. Every MK had at least one opinion , and all were experts on everything

Little has changed today, except that the government is now in the hands of the conservative Likud party. If anything, things are even more contentious. Israel has had six Prime Ministers during the last eight years. In discussing

Israeli politics, one point stands out. With all its faults, Israel was and is, from day-one to the present, a true Western type Democracy. That is a rarity in the Middle East.

Kibbutz in Israel in the early 1950's

BABEL

I indicated earlier that almost everyone I met in Israel spoke English. That is an overstatement, but probably not far from the truth. Early on, the Government decided that, with immigrants arriving from all over the world, the one unifying agent must be a common language, namely Hebrew. Strange to say, Hebrew was not always the language of Jews in the Middle East. Early settlers, before the Zionist movement, were Orthodox Jews who came to Israel to die. Many lived longer than they had thought and even sired children for future generations. Their common language was Yiddish for those of Ashkenazi background and Ladino for those from Sephardic areas. Hebrew was considered a holy language, to be used only for prayer. There are still a few extremely ultra-Orthodox individuals who adhere to this rule.

Hebrew, long an almost dead language, experienced a rebirth in the late 1800's due to the influence of one man, Eliezer Ben-Yehudah. His son was probably the first child in 2,000 years who was raised with Hebrew as a first language. Ben-Yehudah strongly believed that a single language was needed to bring together polyglot Jewish immigrants from many different countries. His arguments were similar to those in U.S. educational circles who oppose bilingualism, insisting that children of recent immigrants be educated in the English language from their first day in school. In spite of opposition from his Orthodox brethren, Ben-Yehudah persisted in proselytizing for Hebrew to be the language of the street as well as in the Synagogue. Obviously, he succeeded.

At the time of my stay in Israel, all immigrants were expected to enroll in Hebrew courses immediately after arrival. Those inducted into the army were required to study Hebrew. Almost all school courses were taught in Hebrew, and many Synagogues had special classes for newcomers. Government-sponsored Hebrew learning centers called Ulpanim could be found all over the country. The pressure for learning Hebrew was so ubiquitous that jokes about it were commonplace. One such story involves an incident in a town called Naharia in the north of Israel, a town which, at that time, had a large community of residents from Germany. Almost everyone spoke German. Two Naharians, strolling along the seashore, heard a drowning swimmer yelling in Hebrew for help. "Ezra! Ezra! Ezra!!" he shouted. "Harrumph," commented one of the men. "Hebrew, he had time to learn, but not enough time to learn how to swim. Let him drown."

Dedicated Israelis spoke Hebrew in their homes, and this was the mother language introduced to their infant children. There were, however, immigrants from many different countries and, while each used his native tongue in talking to his children, the children were also exposed to Hebrew very early in school and in the streets. In addition, most primary schools started teaching English in early grades. Most Americans do not realize that, in a global economy, English can be a valuable tool for educational and commercial advancement. Few Americans speak more than one language well, but residents of smaller nations find English almost indispensable. After all, when you travel or communicate for business purposes, how many people around the world speak Dutch or Danish or Hebrew?

Still, in restaurants, in the streets and in the homes of friends, Israel was a tower of Babel, where most of the major languages of the world could be heard. In multilingual families, two, three or even four languages could be heard during an evening's conversation. It amused me that the language would change as the subjects changed. One tongue might be better suited for discussing politics, another for family matters, and a third for telling jokes.

It also amazed me how many people spoke five or six languages, often quite fluently. Today, I speak French with a formidable American accent and manage some Yiddish. In a limited way, I can also ask directions, order food, exchange a few pleasantries or say, "I love you" in German, Spanish and Hebrew. At that time, however, I was a green, monolingual American, who had spent no time in Europe or other places where many people are multilingual. The ability to master five or six languages was beyond my comprehension. Of course, I was not fully aware of the number of countries where a Wandering Jew (or, more accurately, a fleeing Jew) might have to spend some time before settling safely in Israel.

There were even occasions when one's multilingual knowledge needed to be suppressed. I was once on a "tiul" (casual trip) in northern Israel in a car with three friends. English was our common language, but at least three other languages, including Hebrew, were known by some of us.

We needed to get from Rosh Hanikra on the coast to Kibbutz Ein-Dor, and by far the shortest way was a road running just south of the Lebanese border. Unfortunately, when we got to the road entrance, there was a small sign in Hebrew stating that this was a military road, with no use allowed without a permit. Since reaching our destination by some other route involved going a long way around, we decided to chance it.

About two-thirds of our way, we were stopped by a military patrol car. Our driver cautioned us, "Speak only English." Two soldiers approached and asked us in Hebrew what we were doing on this road. Didn't we see the sign that it was for military use only? "Daber Anglit?" (Do you speak English?) our driver haltingly asked. Fortunately, neither soldier spoke English well. One turned to the other and said in Hebrew that perhaps we had missed the sign. After all, it was small and only in Hebrew. Without thinking, one of us spoke up in English, "Yeah. Why don't you put up a larger sign, in English as well as Hebrew?" We all froze. Fortunately, the soldiers did not catch the significance of the remark and waved us on. We wondered afterwards whether one of them might later have suddenly realized that they had been tricked.

On another occasion, a friend was pulled over by an Israeli policeman for speeding. The officer proceeded to dress him down for going too fast. My friend, who speaks Hebrew fluently, innocently looked up at the policeman and quietly asked, "Do you speak English?" The officer replied, "A leetle," and slowly tried to tell my friend that he had been driving at 100 kilometers per hour. Still appearing innocent, my friend asked in English, "One hundred kilometers? Could you tell me what that is in miles?" The policeman held up his hands in exasperation and waved him on.

To me, the ubiquitousness of English was both a curse and a blessing. It made it much easier for a stranger to get around, but much more difficult to learn Hebrew. After

3 1/2 years in the country, my Hebrew is still limited. There were two reasons. I worked with the Israeli Air Force. In the field of aviation, English is the common language. All pilots, flight attendants, maintenance engineers, flight crew and ground crew speak English. For control tower personnel, English is absolutely essential. Almost everyone I worked with spoke English on the job. Secondly, when I went out on dates with Israeli girls and tried to practice my Hebrew, they all wanted to perfect their English. Since I usually had other things in mind, I never pressed the language point. We spoke English.

Hebrew had been in disuse for 2,000 years. Consequently, it was missing many modern terms, particularly those used in technology. This lead to many amusing concepts. For example, there was no Hebrew word for the back axle of an automobile. So, Israeli mechanics borrowed one from English. They called it the "backaxe." Nor did they have a term for the front axle, so this became the "backaxe kadima." ("Kadima" is Hebrew for "forward.") In other words, the forward back axle. A small panel truck became a "gimcy," since most of their imported panel trucks had been manufactured by <u>G</u>eneral <u>M</u>otors <u>C</u>orporation. Oatmeal was called "kvacker." The only brand they knew was Quaker oats.

It would be a shame to conclude this chapter on languages without telling you one of my favorite true stories about life in Israel. A Welsh friend had a Sabra wife who was a nice lady but terribly naive. While she spoke English, its accuracy left much to be desired. Four of us were traveling in a car and, as usual, we were teasing this lady. We slyly suggested that she had gone to bars to pick up guys to sleep with before she was married. "No," she adamantly protested, "I never had to do that. I had a border." The poor girl couldn't understand why the car suddenly rocked with raucous laughter. What she meant was that, in sexual matters, she had a "limit" beyond which she would not go. What the rest of us heard was that she didn't need to pick up men; she had a "boarder."

THE FAIR SEX

While I was enthusiastic about many new, interesting and exciting experiences in Israel, one unexpected bonus was easy accessibility to numerous attractive young ladies. For a young man of 30, this was indeed a happy hunting ground. As pointed out earlier, Israel at that time was a frontier area with new arrivals every day from Europe, North Africa, Australia, South Africa and the Americas. The new immigrants included a large number of young women.

When I had first moved to New York City ten years earlier, while there were many single women available, meeting them was a problem. Not a difficulty in Israel. All young people were expected to spend time in the military when they reached the age of eighteen. This included women as well as men. Since I was working at one or more Air Force bases and, for six months, was actually stationed at a base, I had ample opportunities to meet members of the fair sex. Relationships among soldiers were very casual, and there was no problem starting conversations which ultimately lead to dates.

Security was very important at the base where I lived, and I needed to show my pass on each entry. So, I was initially concerned as to how to bring a girl to my room if she were a civilian or even if she were a soldier with a pass for another base. No need to worry. Much to my amusement, knowing that we had other things on our minds than espionage, the young soldiers guarding the gate would wave us through, usually with big grins on their faces.

Security, however, was much tighter in other areas. I periodically worked at a military armaments unit on the outskirts of Tel Aviv. Whenever I entered a taxi and gave the name of the base, the driver would feign ignorance and ask me to direct him. It was only when we arrived at our destination that the driver would grin and tell me, "I already knew where this military base is. I just wanted to be sure that you knew."

The Israeli government felt that military service and learning Hebrew were two requirements for integrating immigrants into their new country. To accommodate the large number of newcomers, Ulpanim (special Hebrew schools) were established in different areas of the country. One of the largest was in a resort town called Naharia, a two-hour drive from Tel Aviv.

This area boasted lovely beaches where students spent their spare time. Beaches, of course, are ideal for making casual contacts with women students, most of whom would be living in Tel Aviv after completing their course. Friends and I would drive to Naharia periodically to add names to our little black books.

There were other small schools in Tel Aviv, in one of which I enrolled hoping to improve my Hebrew, among other things. Good contacts were available there also, but you could run into a special problem. Often, entire families were attending the class so, in order to take out a young lady, you needed to meet her father and brothers, who were also classmates. On one occasion, I was two hours late getting my date, a lovely young girl from Egypt, back to her family. My car had been stuck in the sand at Holon, a remote beach area where one could park for a reasonable time without being interrupted. (There were at least three places in Israel where my car had been stuck in sand. Some people will never learn!) At the next class, I was greeted with disapproving looks.

In addition to ease at making contacts, I enjoyed an enviable position when it came to mating and dating. I was considered a much better catch in Israel than in the United States. After my initial six months, I had my own car and my own apartment, both unusual for young Israeli men. And I always had kitchen cupboards full of goodies. Furthermore, my income, which would have been considered reasonably good in New York, was far above the average Israeli salary.

Bringing a car into the country involved heavy import taxes in addition to shipping costs and the price of the car. Consequently, few young people had cars. And, since housing was expensive, most unmarried people lived with their families. My lovely little apartment had one distinctive feature—an entrance door as well as a back door through the kitchen. There were occasions when I was letting someone out the rear door while the bell at the front door was ringing.

An American working in Israel also enjoyed certain psychological advantages in attracting young ladies. In a country where overseas travel was tightly restricted, I was free to come and go. I was working in Israel by choice, not having been forced to emigrate there for political or economic reasons. Finally, I offered a bright future for anyone I might choose to marry, namely the possibility of life in America, something devoutly desired by many young Israelis. In short, when it came to mating and dating, I was in the catbird seat, a position I used to maximum advantage.

If one were looking for variety in women, Israel was ideal. There were young ladies from all over the world. You could find girls from just about every European country, Australia, South Africa, North Africa, various South American countries and several countries in the Middle East, not to mention Americans and Canadians. Oriental women were rare at that time, though several Southeast Asian countries are represented today. There were few black Israelis, but many of the North African and Middle Eastern ladies had tawny complexions. Today, you will find a sampling of black Falashas from Ethiopia.

In spite of their variegated countries of origin, national stereotypical characteristics, strange to say, were infrequently encountered. I once commented on this in a letter to a friend. I told him that I had taken out a Swiss girl who didn't know how to yodel, a Dutch girl who couldn't ice skate and a German girl who hated beer. "It's getting so," I wrote, "that I'm afraid to take out a French girl."

There were some women from small towns and rural areas, what we might call country bumpkins, but most were more sophisticated types with city backgrounds. With the exception of the native born Sabras, they all had one thing in common. All, for a period of time, were strangers in a strange land, a little bit lost, but trying to accommodate and find some stability. Most were relatively free and easy in their relationships with men, not necessarily promiscuous, but with few puritanical hang-ups. Since I rarely took out Orthodox women, I can't speak for them, but almost none of the others were virgins. How to account for this? Possibly the hot climate or the international displacement or the fact that many had served in the Israeli army where men and women were in constant contact. Possibly a more important factor was the fact that they were living in a new country where women (other than those in Orthodox families)were considered to have equal rights to men. If you exclude ultra-Orthodox and Arab women, Israel was and still is a great place for women's liberation.

This last point deserves further elucidation. I had pointed out at the beginning of this book that the Israel of the early 50's was in a sense frontier country, not totally dissimilar to the American West in the late 1800's. Cowboys were the first settlers there, but they were quickly followed by farmers who brought their wives and daughters. Life was hard, and the womenfolk were expected to join the men in farming chores and in bringing in the harvest. History of the American West is replete with stories of tough-minded women. Developing a new U.S. State demanded a new breed of women and a spirit of equality.

Developing the State of Israel demanded a similar equality. Early kibbutz settlements were for the most part farming communities, and many women helped work the fields. Israeli women served early on in the military forces. College education for women was encouraged, and women were welcomed into most professions. Equality of status leads to equality of freedom in sexual as well as in other areas.

I only went out with one Arab girl during my stay in Israel. She was the youngest of seven sisters, holding a full-time administrative job, modern in dress and manner but, with times changing, the first daughter the family allowed to go out with a man unaccompanied by a chaperon. Still, before we could go out for the evening, I had to go to her home and meet her father for a brief conversation. Apparently I passed muster, since he did not object to our going out.

Never before or since have I had so much success with women as I did during my stay in Israel fifty years back. It was a real bonanza, and I made the most of it. After all this time, some of the women I courted there are still friends. After nearly three years of womanizing, it all came to an end. I married a Sabra and brought her back to New York.

Two humorous asides. When I telephoned my mother from Israel to inform her that I was getting married there, she only had one question, "Is she Jewish?" After our wedding celebration, late in the evening, we decided to visit a very good friend who was hospitalized and consequently not able to attend our festivities. It was after visiting hours, but we convinced the nurse attendant that my wife was the sister of the patient who would be horribly disappointed if she could not see her sister in a wedding dress. I, however, was not allowed to go along. Our friend, Irene, takes the story from there. She was lying in a darkened room, half asleep from pain killing drugs, when she saw a wraith-like figure, all in white, coming through the door. Startled, her first thought was, "Oh my God, this is it. My life is over. They've come to take me away."

And a philosophical aside. I married into an Orthodox family, where the father would not even eat in an outside restaurant for fear that its Kashruth was suspect, who regularly and faithfully spent considerable time in the Synagogue, and in whose home the Sabbath was rigidly conducted. It is interesting to note that, over the years, none of the seven sisters and one brother in that family strictly followed the religious precepts of their father. In fact, most live secular lives. In other sections of this book, I point out the growing danger to Israel's secular government resulting from a huge discrepancy in the size of Orthodox and secular families. The situation with my former in-laws illustrates a possible counterweight to this trend.

Getting back to the subject of the fair sex, before concluding this chapter, I might comment that, at the time of my stay in Israel, there was no prostitution. One early Israeli sage commented that Israel would not become a modern nation until there were Jewish beggars, thieves, and prostitutes. If he were alive today, he would find that Israel is now, without question, a modern nation.

"TIULIM" — EXPLORING ISRAEL

Since my job in Israel, I have become an international traveller, spending time in over 70 countries. Friends often ask my advice on the best destinations for the traveller with only one or two weeks to spend on the road. I always recommend two places—Italy and Israel. In both of these countries, a tourist can see many wonderful scenes without wasting too much time travelling long distances between interesting and exciting sites or events.

That is the advice I give today. Fifty years ago, while there were many places worth visiting in Israel, the country was not yet ready for the traveller hoping to see everything comfortably without too much strain and effort. With a few major exceptions such as the King David Hotel in Jerusalem, hotel facilities were limited. Furnishings in most hotels could best be described as spartan. Air conditioning was not exactly ubiquitous, a major problem in a hot country. Very few quality restaurants existed, and food standards were way below normal tourist expectations.

Moreover, many of the wonderful archeological sites requiring years and years of excavation were not fully developed, not quite ready for easy viewing. Roads leading to many interesting areas were not properly paved, and helpful safety signals and signposting were just beginning to be developed. While driving on a country road one evening, I nearly ran into two camels being led along the road. Neither had tail lights. Toilet facilities were primitive, and a large percentage of toilets were those common in Arab countries; instead of having a toilet seat, you had to stand on two raised footprints, squat and aim at a hole between the steps.

In short, tourism in Israel and even ""tiulim" (brief road trips) were for the hardy and for young people toting back packs and not expecting posh sleeping quarters. For those of us living there at the time, however, particularly if you had a car at your disposal, it was paradise. Almost every Friday afternoon, friends and I would take off on a tiul for some place or other we had heard about. This included Jerusalem, Arab villages, unspoiled beaches, out-of-the-way towns and settlements, lively kibbutzim and interesting archeological sites. The digs were not anywhere as developed as they are today, but one didn't need to bother with fences, ticket booths and large crowds. It was almost as if these fascinating places had been reserved solely for the enjoyment of my friends and me. Sort of like a private dining room for a tryst.

One of the first places we visited was Nazareth, reportedly the home of Mary and Joseph and the scene of

Tiberias and the Sea of Galilee

Jesus' early years. For today's tourists, particularly those of a religious bent, Nazareth boasts a number of important churches, including the Basilica of the Annunciation, a magnificent structure containing a large collection of mosaics and icons associated with the birth of Christ. The Basilica had not been completed at the time of my early visits, but the Grotto of the Annunciation, over which the Basilica is built, and the adjacent ruins of a Crusader church provided an intriguing site for a young American's first view of a truly Arab town. This was the first of many archeological and religious sites I was able to take in weekend after weekend.

Perhaps more interesting from a human point of view was the old city of Nazareth itself. This mostly Arab city is relatively small, but provided a visitor a view of life in an Arab town as contrasted with life in Tel Aviv or Haifa. Narrow streets, timeworn buildings, and a slower pace of life. A lively population, crowded and noisy "sooks" (market areas) and many small restaurants with their tempting odors. Souvenir shops marketing religious icons, hand hammered brass pots, handmade lace and bric-a-brac galore. A local population with a wide variety of garb—modern dress, burnooses, kaftans, clerical habit, robes, cloaks, cowls and kaffiyehs. It had ancient roots, but to me, it was all new.

Old painting of the Western Wall in Jerusalem

To add salt to the scene, there was the ubiquitous religious life. A church almost everywhere you turned; the wail of the muezzin high up in his minaret, anachronistically using a modern loud-speaker to summon the faithful to prayer; the faithful prostrating themselves while facing Mecca, shouting "Allehu Akbar," (Allah is greatest), the sound penetrating every street and alleyway. One Christmas, I attended mass in Nazareth, experiencing a beautiful but totally different ceremony than those I had previously witnessed in New York. This first visit to Nazareth was more than fifty years ago, but I remember it vividly.

Many other significant ruins and archeological sites provided key destinations for weekend wandering during my three years in the infant state of Israel. As previously noted, most of the ruins and archeological sites were in primitive condition, having for the most part been ignored for 2,000 years. Today, Israel leads the world with the highest per capita rate of archeological excavations and expeditions. Many Israelis, then and now, were part-time archeological buffs. This included Moshe Dayan, a well-known general and popular political figure. Fifty years back, my friends and I experienced our own mini-expeditions to many sites, some of which involved driving over unpaved or badly paved roads in order to reach them. I often felt sorry for my automobile.

Haifa at night, overlooking the Mediterranean Sea

There were so many archeological treasures that it is difficult to remember them all, but certain highlights quickly come to mind. The second century Capernaum Synagogue on the northern shore of the picturesque Sea of Galilee, also known as Lake Kinneret, was one of these. It was built over a previous synagogue, where Jesus preached sermons. Capernaum was said to be Jesus's second home. Visiting the port of Caesarea, we explored the remains of a Roman theater and ruins left behind by the Crusaders. Ruins in the city of Ashkalon boasted a beautiful marble statue of the Greek Goddess of Victory. Along the northern border with Lebanon, we discovered the remains of the Bar-Am Synagogue, where Queen Esther is reputed to be buried. In ancient Beit Shean, ignoring the intense heat, we marvelled at Roman mosaics, amazingly in almost as good shape as they were 2,000 years ago.

Then there was Masada, a huge boulder near the Dead Sea, with fascinating historical significance. Only one tortuous narrow path led to the top. Climbing it was not like conquering Everest but, in Israel's extreme heat, believe me, it required a major sweaty effort and a lot of time. Reaching the top made it all worthwhile. The views in all directions were fabulous. And we were able to explore extensive ruins, including those of King Herod's castle, with its mosaic floors and adjoining swimming pool. Less decorative but more intriguing were the deep cisterns for storing rain water, since no other water sources were available. The foundations of large storage rooms for food were also evident. It boggles the mind to imagine the difficulties of bringing building materials and supplies up the single narrow pathway. Today, tourists have the advantage of a cable car ride to the top, but our small group of explorers had to mount the rock the hard way, the same way the early Zealots did.

Masada is one of the most historical sites in Israel. Originally built by master builder King Herod about 35 B.C., control of the site changed hands several times between then and 70 A.D., when it was captured by a religious community called the Zealots. At that time, the Romans had conquered virtually all of what is now Israel, and Masada remained the last stronghold. All this provides the basis of a tragedy, which remains an integral part of Israeli history, myth spirit and pride.

Masada remained the only place the Romans had not captured, which stuck in their craw for several years until a Roman general, Flavius Silva, decided to finish the job. He first tried surrounding the rock and putting it under siege, hoping that the Zealots would soon capitulate to hunger and thirst. The defenders managed to find ways around this strategy, so Silva tried another tack, this time successfully. He ordered a huge ramp to be built against the western slope to provide access for his troops. The ramp was strong enough to support heavy duty catapults and a battering ram to knock down the defending walls. This was a major undertaking which consumed more than a year, but ultimately succeeded. Vestiges of the ramp are still visible to tourists.

What makes the defense of Masada more than just another conquest story is that, once defeat by the Romans became evident, the Zealots decided that they would all commit suicide instead of surrendering. The story goes that over a thousand people were killed by their husbands and fathers, and that the last ten men drew lots to determine the order in which they would die. The final survivor committed suicide. When the Roman soldiers knocked down or scaled the walls, all they encountered was dead silence and dead bodies. They were deprived of their normal slaughter ritual and victory celebration. In a kind of Pyrrhic victory, they met defeat, at least psychologically.

Israelis attribute their present day victories against much larger Arab armies to the spirit of Masada. Victory or annihilation were their only two choices. Whenever I visited Masada, I was aware, not only of the ruins, but also of the ghosts of the defiant Zealots lingering at the site.

Visible from the top of Masada is the Dead Sea, which provided another worthwhile visiting site. Since the Dead Sea is the lowest body of water on earth, there is no outlet for its waters. Only evaporation keeps the Sea level from rising, and this evaporation over centuries has created an extremely dense, very salty lake. We all tried swimming in the Dead Sea, but this was impossible. The salt concentration is so high that one must be very careful to protect one's eyes. It also makes the Sea so dense and buoyant that it is impossible to sink. We had fun sitting up in the water with our heads well out of reach of the caustic salt. We even saw one "bather" reading a newspaper while floating. Unfortunately, this water can be very irritating if allowed to dry on the skin. All of us had to climb quickly to a nearby spring in order to thoroughly rinse off all the salt. There were no showers available there at that time.

During my stay, and even today, the *pièce de résistance* for any tiulim in Israel was the City of Jerusalem. Not only did it boast a large number of important archeological sites, but the city itself was a delight to visit. I doubt if we saw all the twelve gates of Jerusalem, but we did visit the more important ones—the Jaffa gate, the Damascus gate, the sealed Golden gate, the Lions gate and the Zion gate. We walked the walls. We watched Jews at prayer at the Western Wall. We gaped at the white Dome of the Rock, from which Mohammed ascended to Heaven, according to Muslim belief.

Putting history and archeology aside, Jerusalem in its way is one of the most beautiful cities in the world. Situated atop a group of hills, it commands absorbing views in all directions. Virtually all buildings are made of local stone, which provides a harmonious distinctiveness that no other city in the world possesses. The modern part of the city can boast wide boulevards and lovely gardens. In contrast, the Old City has an exotic quality with its narrow lanes lined with Arab shops of all varieties, with their proprietors determinedly hawking business. The Old City is also famous for ancient churches and mosques, including the Church of the Holy Sepulcher and the El-Aqsa Mosque.

Jerusalem is known as the center of the world's three largest religions, so it is not surprising today to find over fifty different mosques and churches of many denominations in a relatively small city. Most of these were there during my early visits. Today's visitors will find a larger modern city with enough museums, monuments and other sites to satisfy the most ardent tourist.

There was so much to see in my spare time that I could write an entire book on Israeli tourism, but that is not this book. In addition to all of the above, we were able to enjoy pristine sandy beaches stretching in both directions without having to put up with noisy crowds. Great care had to be taken if you wanted to swim. There were dangerous undertows and no lifeguards. We were welcomed to a number of kibbutzim, which offered us lunch and guided tours. We viewed intriguing spots such as the entrance to a train tunnel at Rosh Hanikra on the Israeli-Lebanese border, the former rout of one branch of the famous Oriental Express, now completely sealed at both ends. Some of the roads we travelled, now well-paved, were one- or two-lane dirt tracks, e.g. the old road to Safed. Some were still dangerous. On the old road to Jerusalem, one could see signs of the last war, wrecks of cars, trucks and tanks visible on both sides.

We made regular visits to the ancient city of Akko, a walled town of great historical interest, mostly populated by Arabs at that time, and even today with a large Arab population. Many small but good Arab restaurants kept attracting us. We spent time in Israel's most modern city, Haifa, and in exploring nearby Mount Carmel. Had I had foresight, I would have bought land there, very cheap at the time but now expensive, since it provides attractive suburban residences for many commuters who work in Haifa. And we occasionally travelled to Israel's Negev desert, which Mark Twain once described as "a desolation that not even imagination can grace with the pomp of life and action." Still, it had its own magnificence. There were signs that people had once lived there, as evidenced by culverts and caves designed to store water during rainy periods.

Since the State of Israel was less than 300 miles long and, at some places, no more than 20 miles wide, it was relatively easy to explore. For this young man with no prior experience overseas, Israel offered the chance to wander and wander, constantly viewing a wealth of scenes and sights and situations beyond anything he could possibly have previously imagined.

Arab village in the Galilee

BEST OF ALL, THE PEOPLE

I cherish many fond memories of my 3 1/2 years in Israel fifty years ago, but the best ones are reserved for the people I met. Many were pioneers hoping to resurrect a state which had been moribund for 2,000 years. Others came to Israel, not out of choice, but because they were victims of the Holocaust and had no other place to go. Many of these would have preferred to emigrate to the United States, but lacked visas. Some aging Orthodox Jews came to Israel to die.

I spoke to two American immigrants who were super-sensitive to what they considered anti-semitism at home, real or imagined. I personally had never had that problem, so either I was lucky or just thick-skinned. However, I know a Thai gentleman, a former member of their parliament, who had lived in physical comfort in America for years, but returned home because of stressful contacts with anti-Asian bigots. So, maybe I was missing something. I met one woman, a former German Christian who had converted to Judaism as a protest against Hitler's pogroms.

I spent time with people from over fifty different countries. They were an odd lot. A Swedish Jew who spoke both English and Yiddish with a thick Swedish accent we found hilarious. Israelis who knew English but refused to speak it because they were so pissed-off at the British for their pro-Arab activities. In the same vein, I have since encountered people in India who had found British occupation so abominable they refused to speak the language of their persecutors. Orthodox Ashkenazic Jews whose families originated in eastern Europe. Sephardic Jews of Spanish or Portuguese descent. Israelis who practiced many variations of their religion or none at all.

There were soldiers, known as Mahalnicks, who had fought with the British army in Africa or the Air Force in Europe who, on being discharged, immediately joined the Israeli military. Some of these were soldiers of fortune; the only life they knew involved combat. Most were dedicated to building a Jewish homeland. I became friendly with many young native born Israelis. And then there were others who, like myself, came as hired specialists needed to do certain jobs where local skills were not available. Some of us remained after our contracts were up.

In other words, a mishmash of people, all of whom, happily or unhappily, were working together to establish a viable state and fulfill a 2,000-year-old dream. I mingled with all of them, liked some, disliked others and did not know enough about many to form an opinion. Some were exciting, some dull and most about average. They constituted a cross section similar what you might find in New York. However, I came away with two distinct opinions.

The first deals with spirit. Israel today is essentially the equivalent of an American state. Israelis are a lively bunch, intelligent, gregarious, hardworking and ambitious. Most Americans, particularly our city dwellers, would feel at home there. Were it not for the never-ending battle with the Arabs, the Israelis would be enjoying a good life. While I was there over fifty years back, life was nowhere near as good from a material point of view. There were many hardships and discomforts. *La dolce vita* did not exist. But the **spirit**, the spirit was as high among the populace as anywhere in the world I have ever been. People worked together, helped each other, made do with whatever they could find. It was more than just cooperation. It was a concentrated joint striving towards a common goal. Were there arguments and differences? Plenty. But the vision of a new and successful country and a bright future never dimmed.

Rarely have I seen such profuse cooperation back home, with two notable exceptions. One occurred many years back, when there was an eleven-day transit strike. The other event was during an extended power blackout, when elevators in high-rise buildings were no longer functioning. The bottom line is that tragedy brings us all together, whatever our creed or nationality. People are never nicer than during times where they really need one another.

A second opinion. Call it prejudice if you wish, but I really liked the immigrant population much more than the native born Sabras. The immigrants seemed to have wider interests and were more culturally aware. They were perpetually argumentative on a wide variety of subjects, but they at least had some knowledge of these subjects. While they may have from time to time been irritating, most of them were rarely dull. For me, rapport with these people came easy. The Sabras had a sharper edge to them, bordering on arrogance, perhaps an undeserved arrogance. Their banner could well have been an early American flag showing a coiled snake, with the message, "Don't Tread on Me." If I were to search for a single word to describe them, it would be "brash." Of course there were exceptions in both groups. It is not that the Sabras were bad or obstreperous. It was simply that, with my background, I felt more at home with their parents and grandparents. One might easily argue that the Sabra temperament was a necessary development to handle the trials and tribulations they were about to face.

Over 80 years, I have met hundreds, perhaps thousands of interesting people all over the world, but never have I found so many concentrated in a small country such as Israel.

Best of all were the numerous close friends I gathered during my stay in Israel, some of whom remain friends to

UPDATING

Lots of water has run under the bridges over the Yarkon River since the time I spent there. The Israeli population has swelled enormously, fed by waves of immigrants from Europe, America, Canada, North Africa, South Africa, Australia, Ethiopia, other Middle Eastern states and, more recently, Russia. It is now over 6.5 million, perhaps ten times as large as it was during my stay. The infrastructure is now up-to-date, with properly paved roads, busy airports, a railroad, an excellent water and sewage system and modern electrical and telephone lines.

Tel Aviv is a metropolis. It competes with many of the world's cities in its crowded roads and traffic jams. If you have the money, you can buy almost anything in its fashionable shops. The sandy beachfront regularly attracts swimmers and loungers. There are theaters, museums and art galleries and a wide variety of restaurants to suit every ethnic taste, including Indian, Chinese and Japanese.

Commercially, the country has thrived. In addition to citrus, Israel now exports fruits, vegetables and flowers of every variety. Electronics and computer companies have thrived, as have the diamond and pharmaceutical industries. Until the recent Intifada, the tourist industry had been a major moneymaker. The airport is a port of call for airlines of many countries.

All of this has happened in spite of four additional wars with neighboring Arab states—the Sinai Campaign of 1956, the Six-Day War of 1967, the Yom Kippur War of 1973 and the Lebanese War in 1982. During these wars, Israel suffered considerable losses but ultimately prevailed, more than doubling the size of the state in the process. The population continued to increase, though there has been a growing exodus as well. Many Americans and Europeans who helped build the country went back to their native lands. Over one million Sabras left to seek greener pastures elsewhere.

In spite of its military victories, Israel has unfortunately never been able to achieve peace with its neighbors. Frankly, the area was more peaceful during my stay than it is now. The absence of war has prevailed over intermittent periods of varying lengths, but regular uprisings continue. The recent Intifada has probably been the worst. Horrifying but ineffectual suicide bombings against civilians have resulted in the deaths of more than a thousand Israelis. Military counterattacks and reoccupation of Arab villages have undoubtedly reduced the number of suicide bombings but have stirred up more anger on both sides. No end seems to be in sight.

Tourists may hesitate to visit Israel under these circumstances but, peculiarly, those who do visit see few signs of war unless they visit border areas. Day to day life goes on pretty much as usual. Unfortunately, however, an underlying feel of nervousness hangs over everyone.

Predicting the future is always treacherous. In spite of the fact that all peace attempts have failed, common sense dictates that, sooner or later, fatigue will set in and a settlement will be reached. We live in hope. I, however, have another fear. Two of Israel's strengths are that it is a democracy and that it has a secular government. Both are threatened in a long-term scenario. As in all countries with a high standard of living, the birth rate among average Israelis has declined. Two or three children is the norm. Among Arab Israelis, however, five to ten children is not unusual. Over a long period, the Arab population could overwhelm the Jewish population, and Israel might have to choose between remaining a democracy or losing its Jewish character. A more imminent threat is to the secular nature of the country. Orthodox Jewish families also raise large numbers of children, and a majority of voters may well favor the Orthodox viewpoint in the not-too-distant future. I personally strongly favor a strict division between church and state.

For the present, however, in spite of its many trials and tribulations, today's State of Israel is in good shape. On my more-or-less annual visits there, I still like the country, and I still feel at home there. I must say, however, that, while I very much like Israel now, fifty years ago I really loved it.

It may seem odd to the reader that I express love for a place where I experienced so many frustrations. I started this book saying that I would offer neither a sycophantic portrayal nor a highly critical view of Israel. I have tried to do so but, as I reread my text, it occurs to me that I may have told too many critical anecdotes and not enough stories about the joys experienced during my three and a half years of living there. There is a reason for this. Perhaps, as with individuals, e.g. Julius Caesar, negative memories persist, while the good ones are interred.

An alternative explanation is more likely. The fact is that so many of the irritating or confusing or frustrating events described made for good storytelling, both to friends at the time and to present readers. The occurrences may have rubbed me the wrong way but, in retrospect, they are interesting or amusing. The positive things that happened were more diffuse. They consisted, not so much in specific incidents, as in daily routines involving friendships, exploration, discovery, discussions and laughter, not to mention a real sense of achievement in what I accomplished during my stay. I may have contributed only a smidgeon towards the building of a new country, but I know that I did make a contribution, even if a small one.

Suffice it to say that, in spite of any complaints I may have had, I really enjoyed my stay in Israel. I loved the Country, and I love my memories of the time spent there.

FINAL THOUGHTS

Just as many changes have occurred in Israel during the fifty years or so since I returned to the United States, many things have happened to me as well. I have aged from 30 to 81, hopefully grown more mature and wiser. Sometimes for pleasure but more often on business, I have travelled worldwide to over 70 countries and 49 American states, many of them on numerous occasions.

In addition to Israel, I have lived for extended periods of time in New York, California, London and Bangkok. By nature, I am curious, so my visits to many places were not just casual tourist trips nor business quickies. I made many long-term friends en route and tried to immerse myself in local culture and familiarize myself with the local environment, both in major cities and in the countryside. While New York City and America remain my spiritual home, I feel at home almost everywhere. This may sound smug, but I think of myself as a citizen of the world.

Having said all that, I still think of Israel as someplace *sui generis*, something special. Intellectually, I know that many cities and countries have myriad advantages over Israel, particularly when it comes to material benefits, but emotionally, there is still an intense tug at the heart. Perhaps, having spent time there in its infancy, I see Israel, not as the grown-up country it is now, but as the infant I used to know and love. The three and a half years I spent there were indeed a feather in my yarmulke.